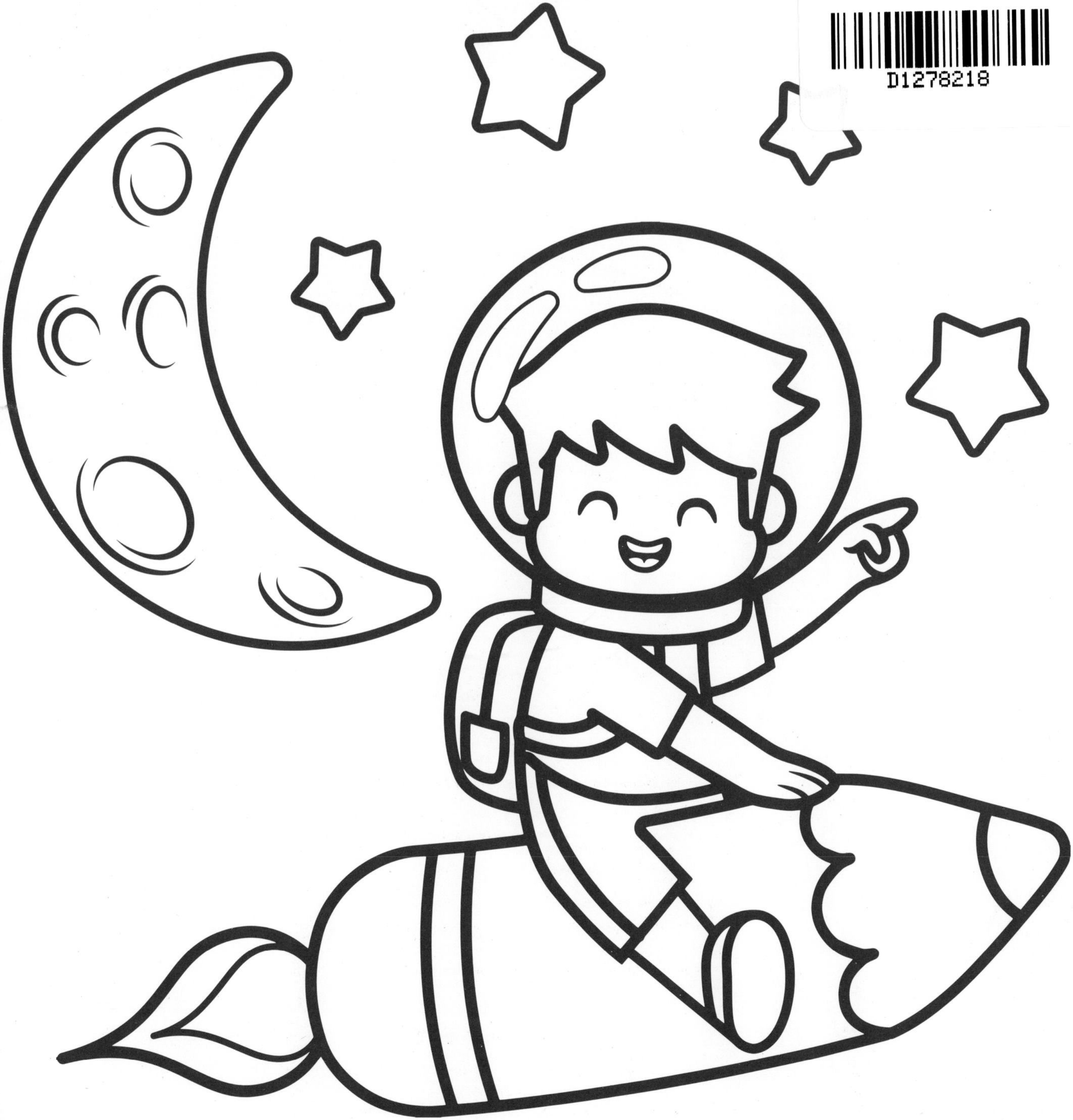

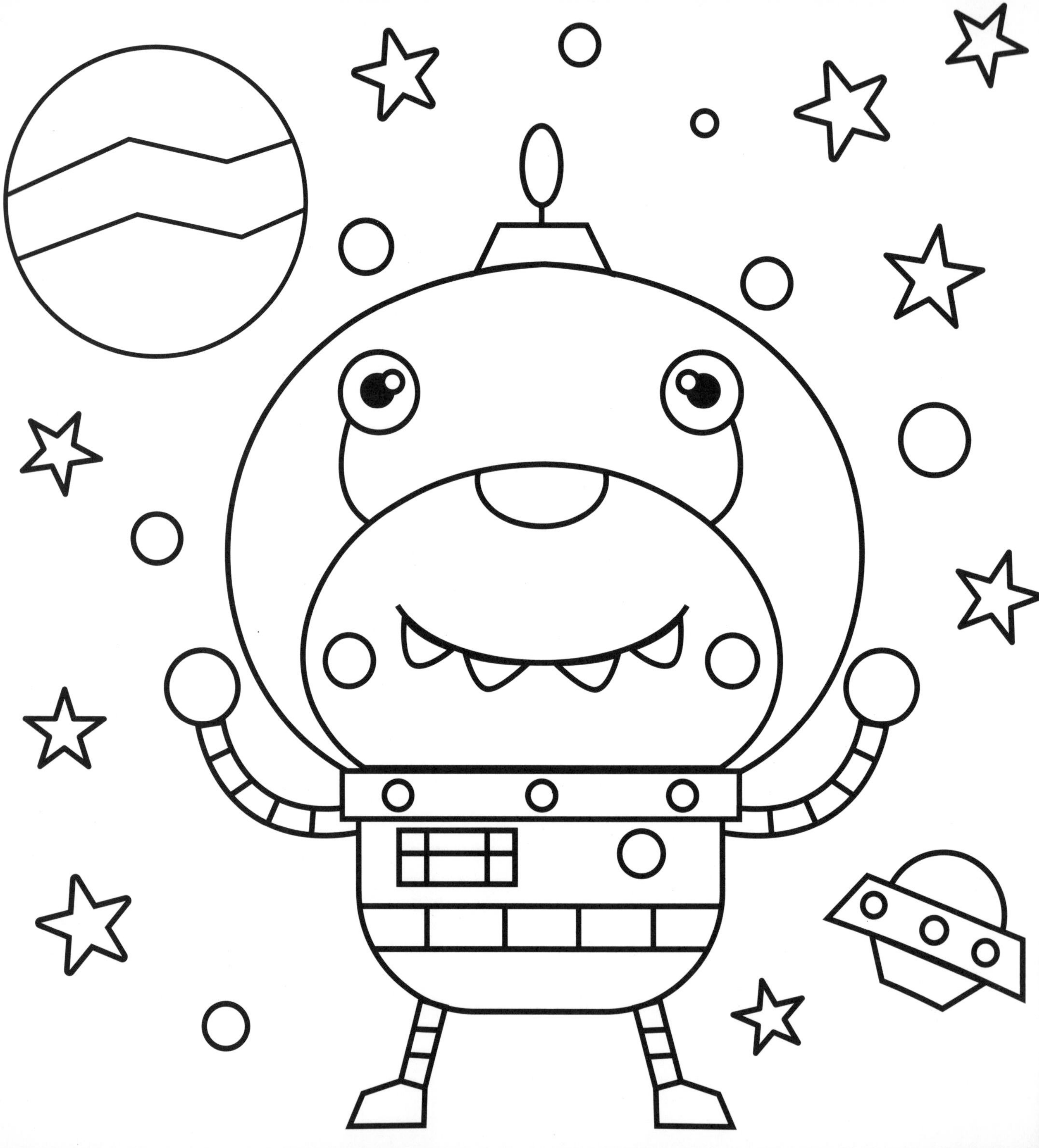

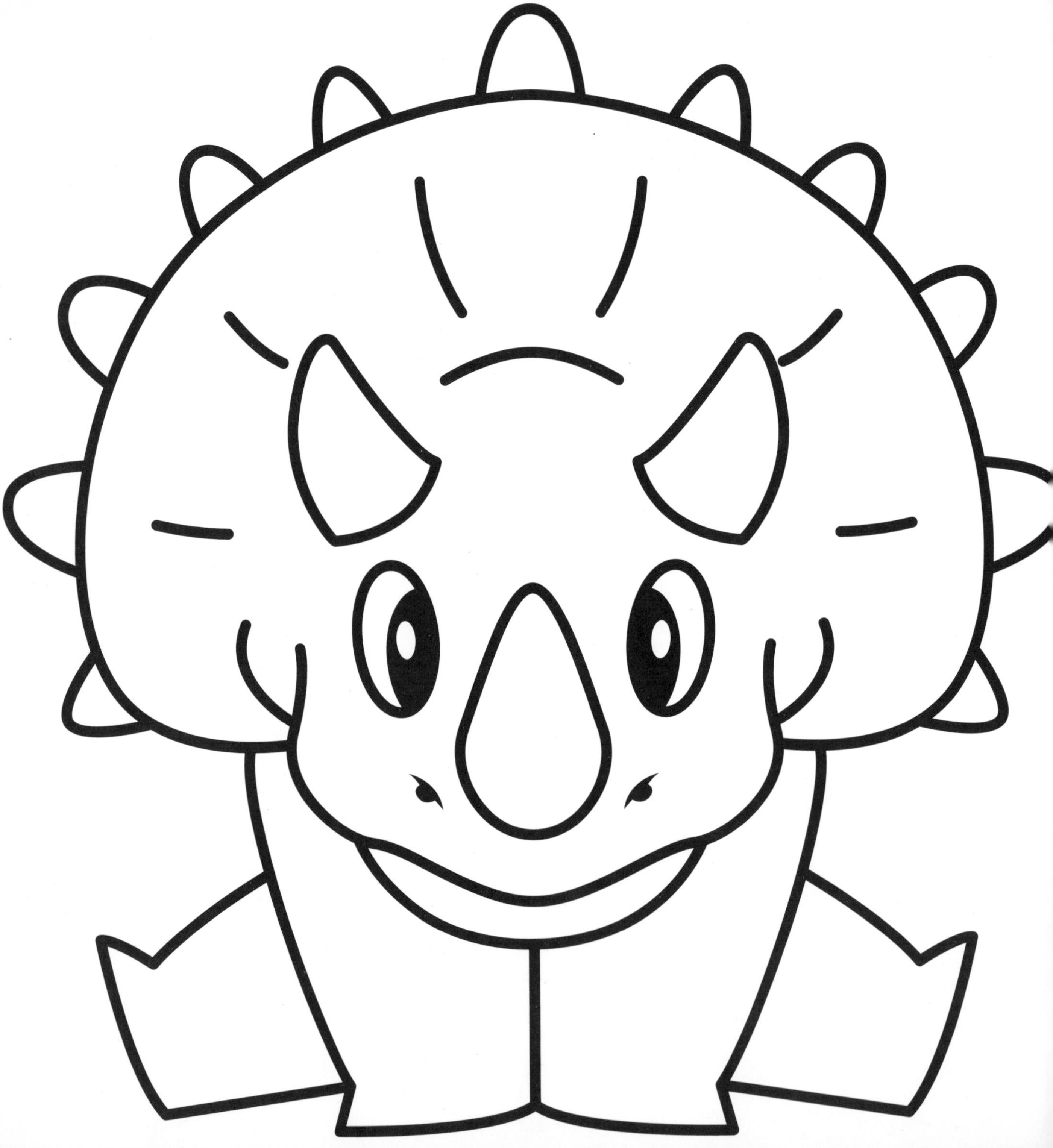

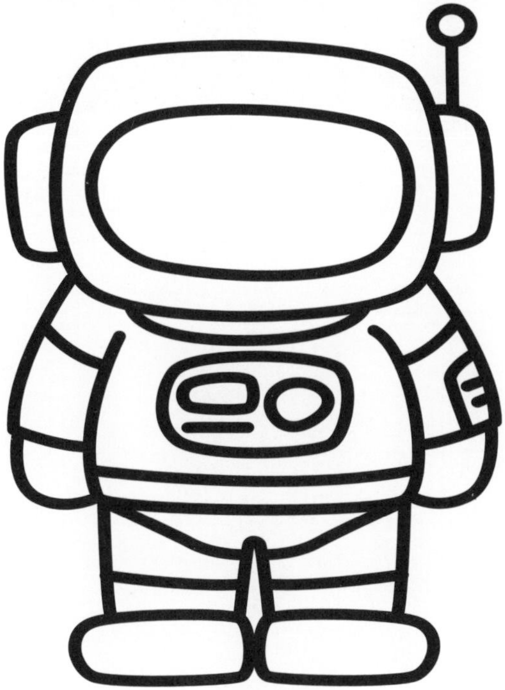

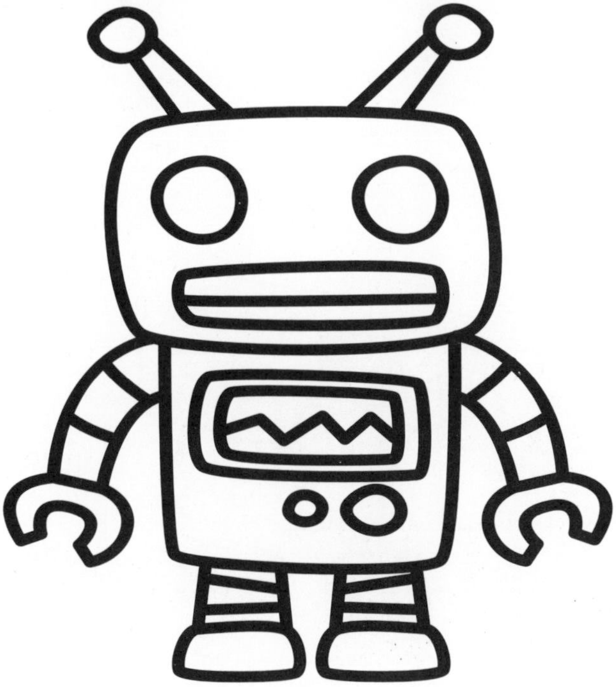

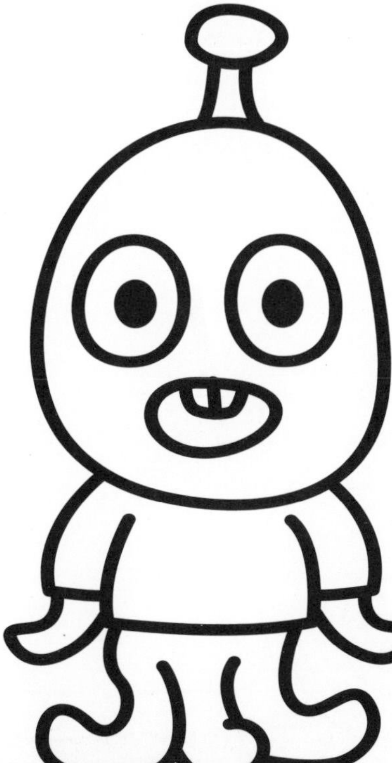

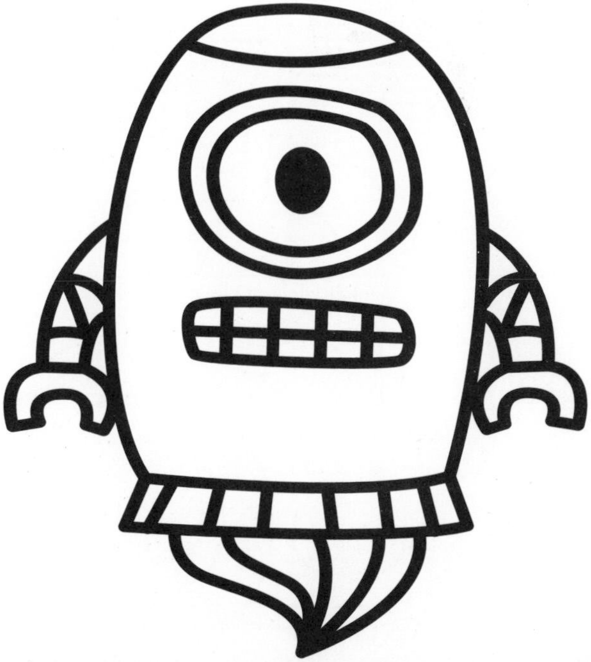

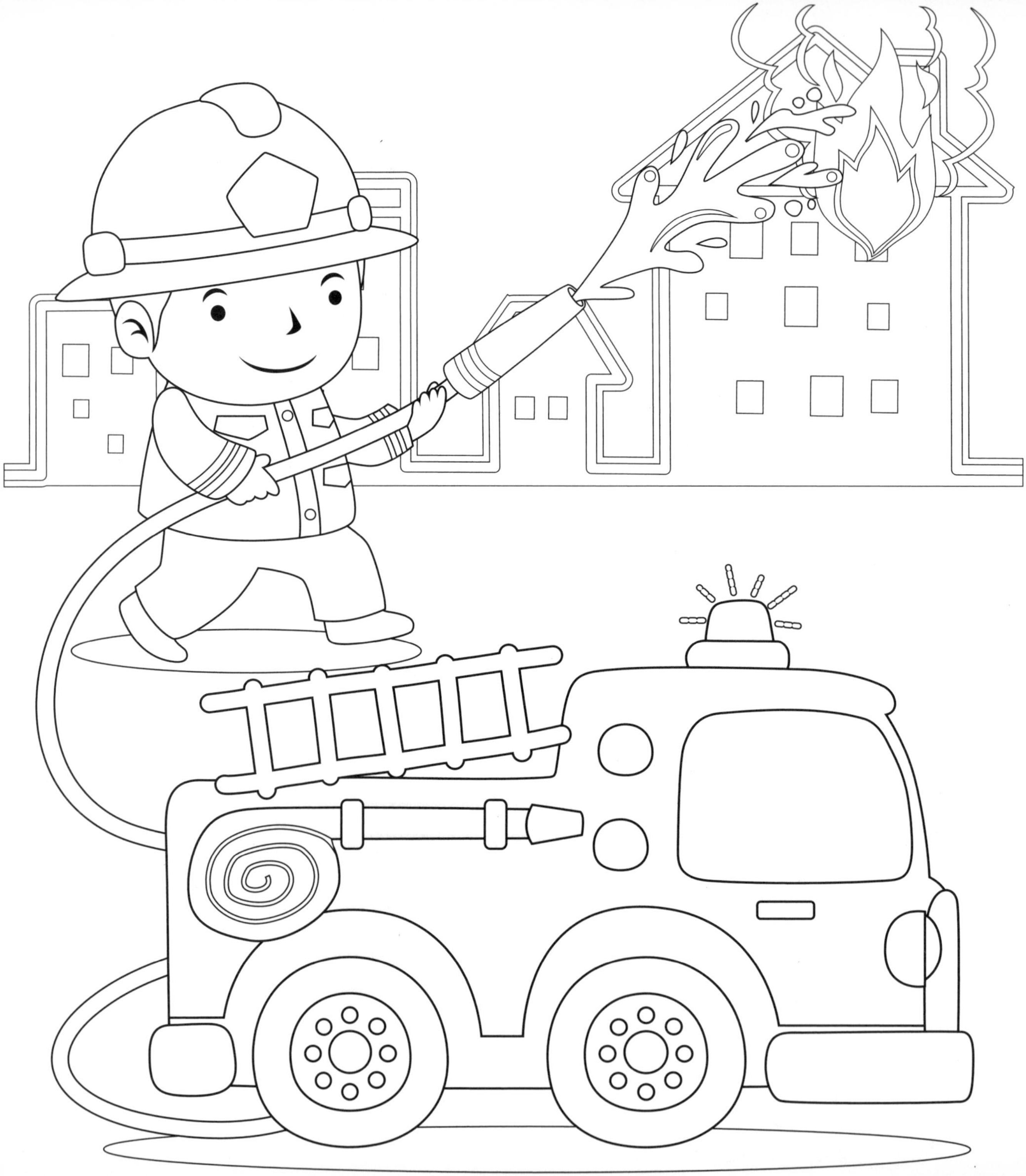

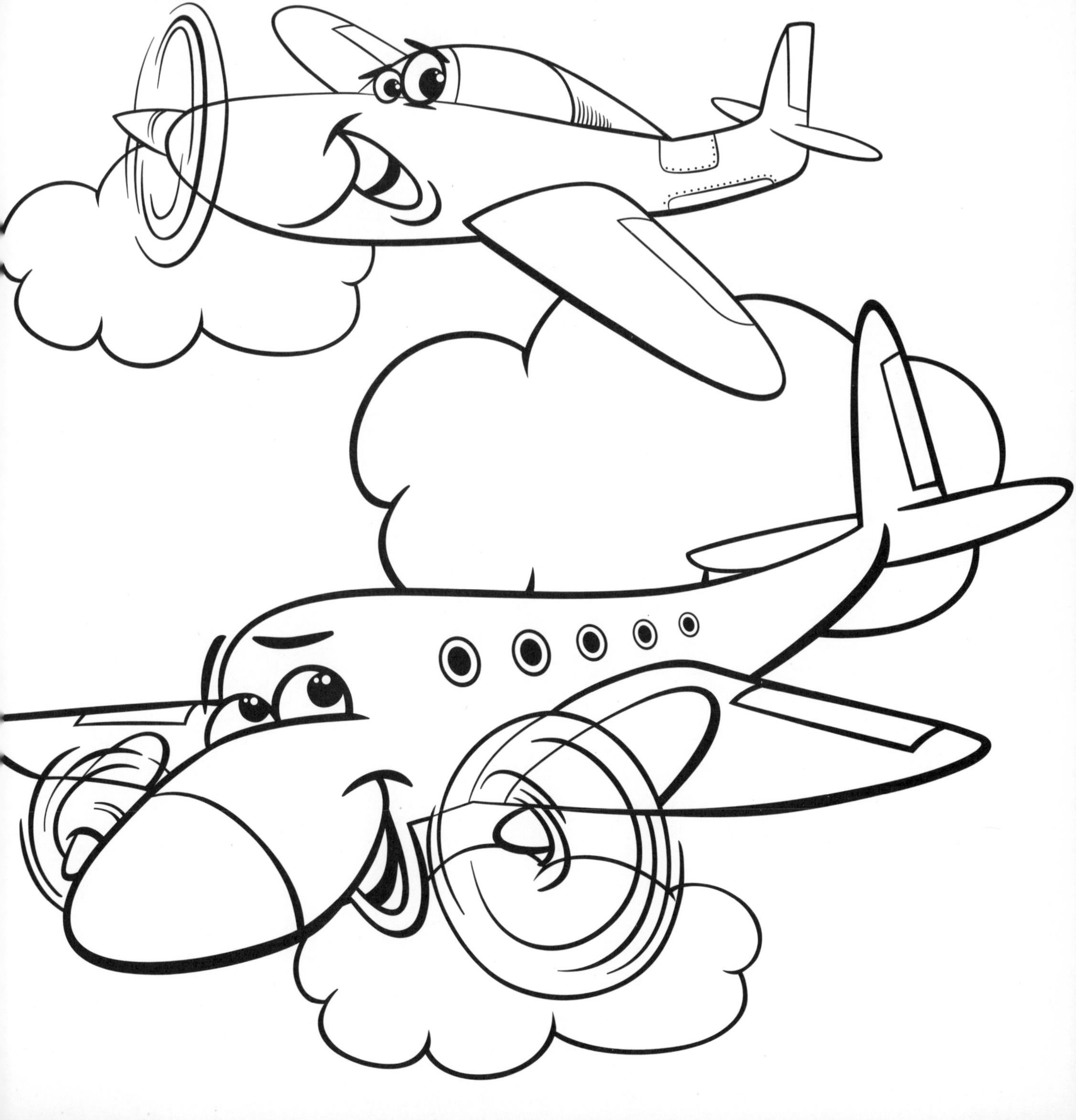

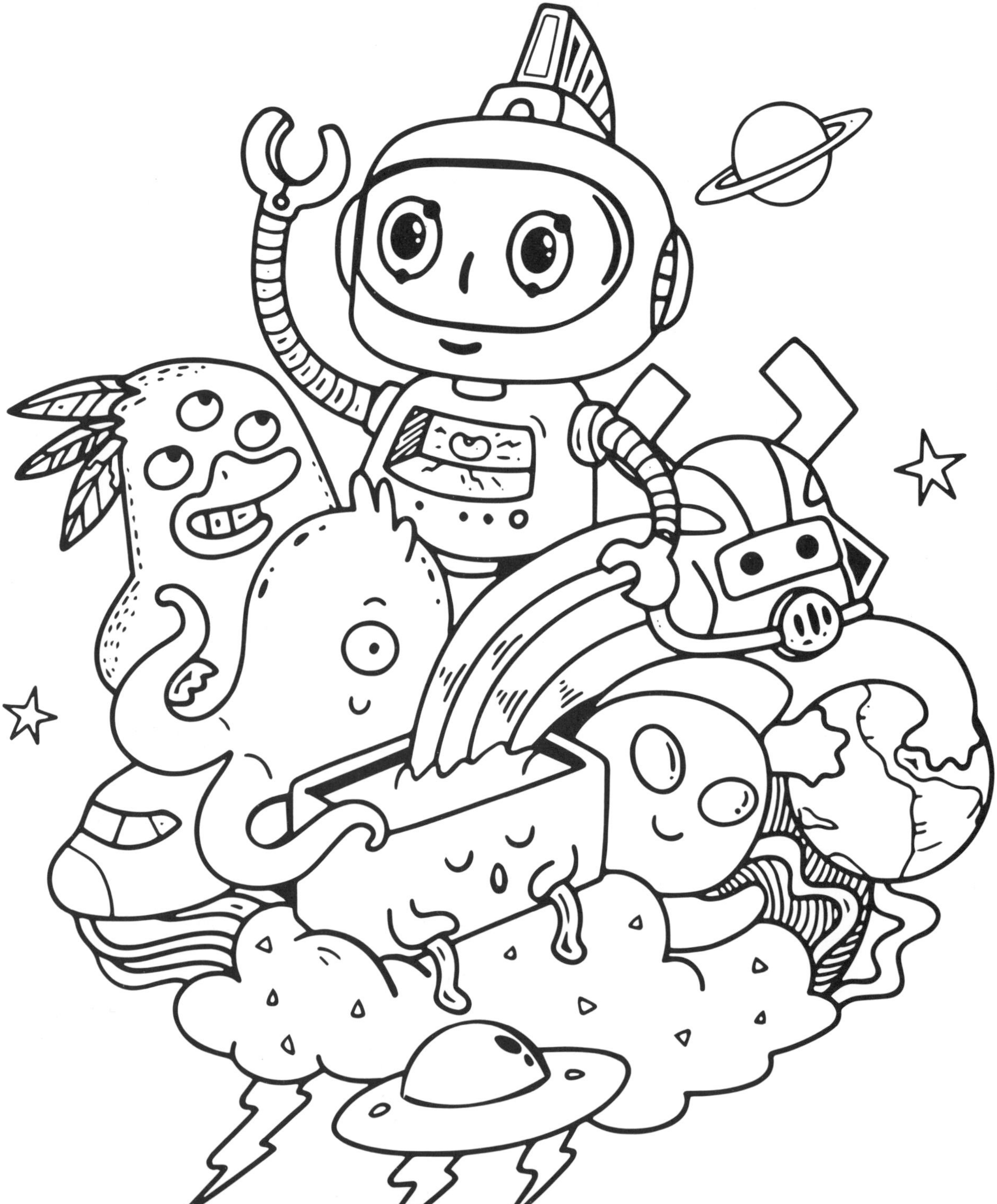

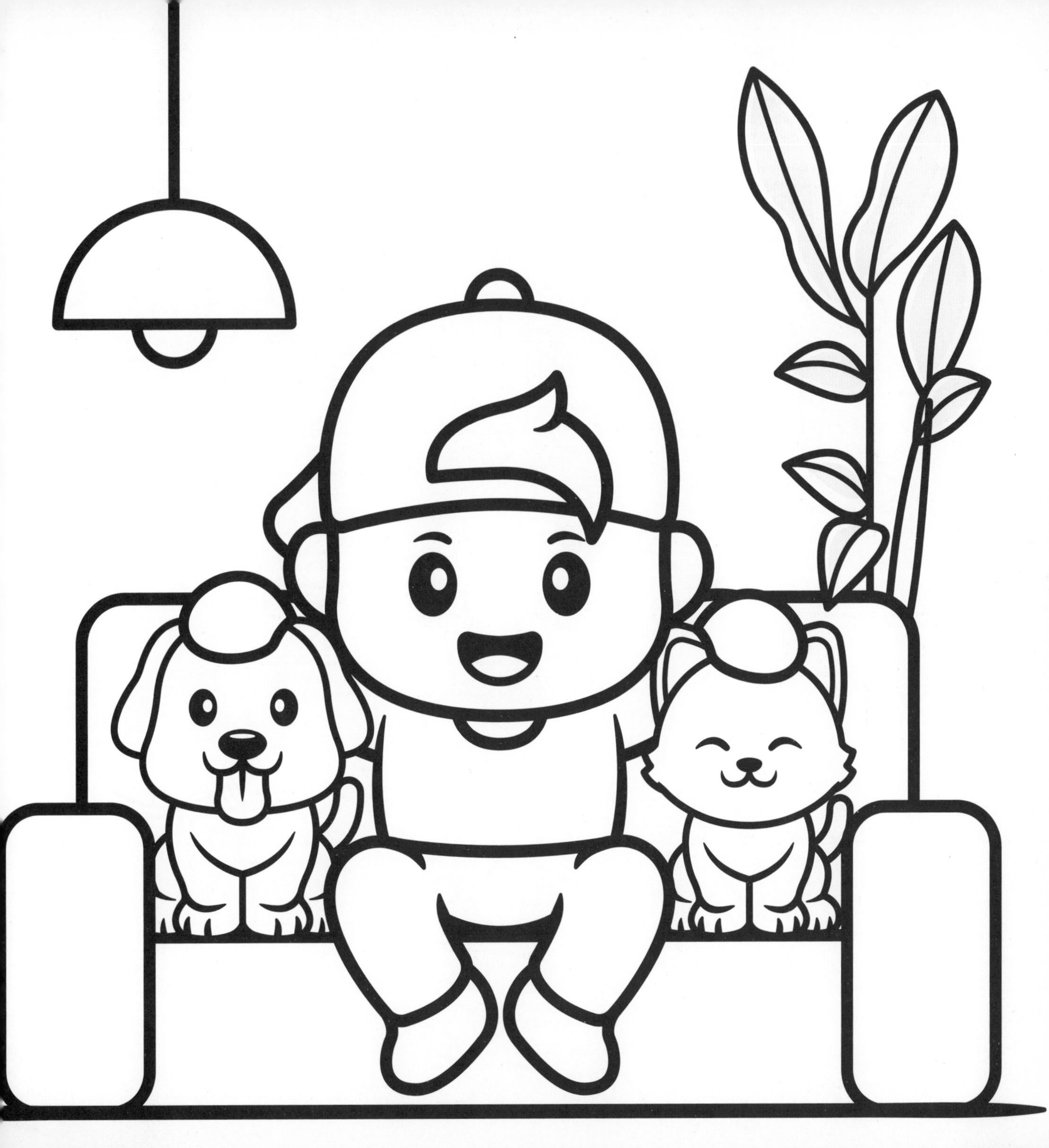

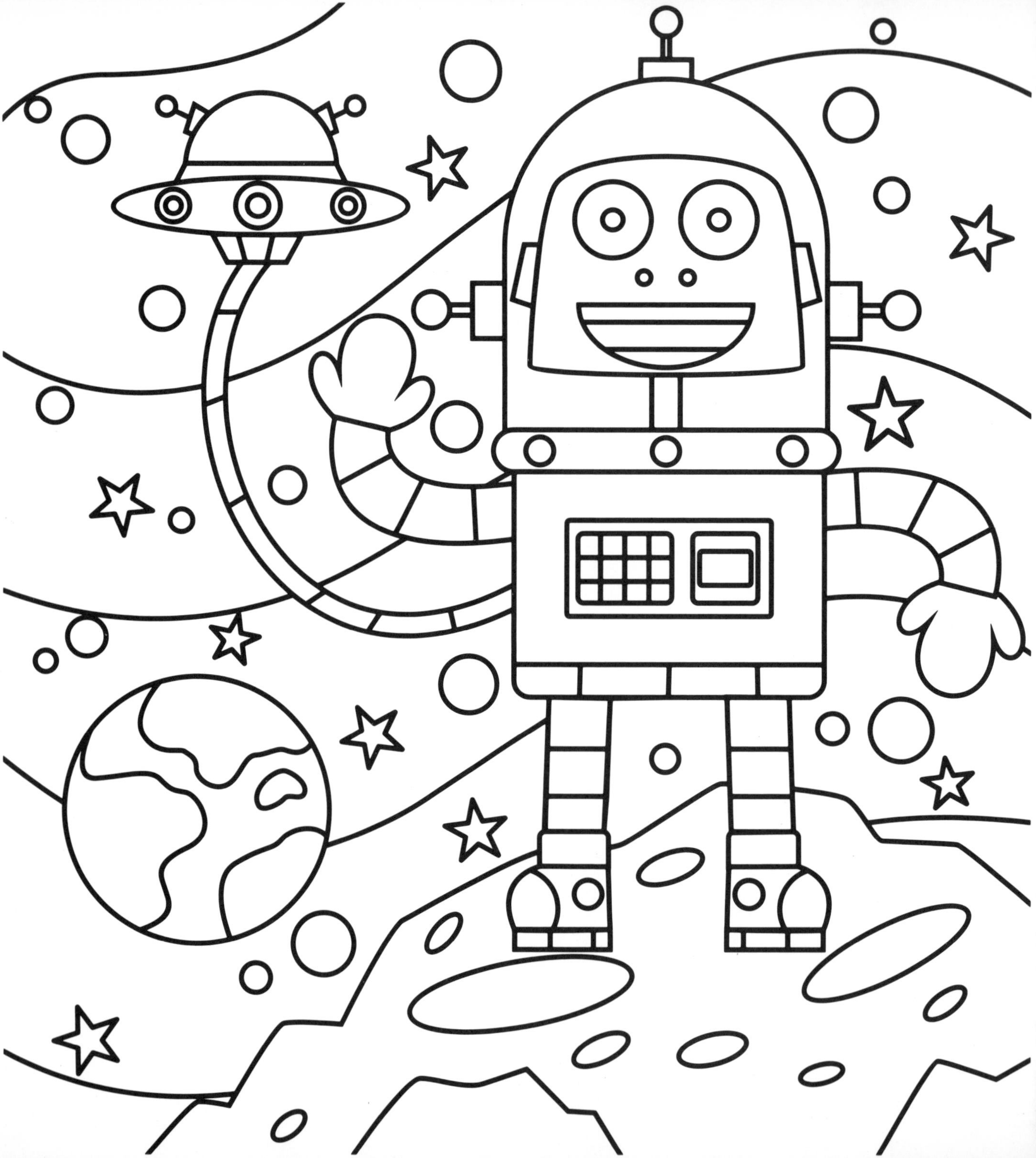

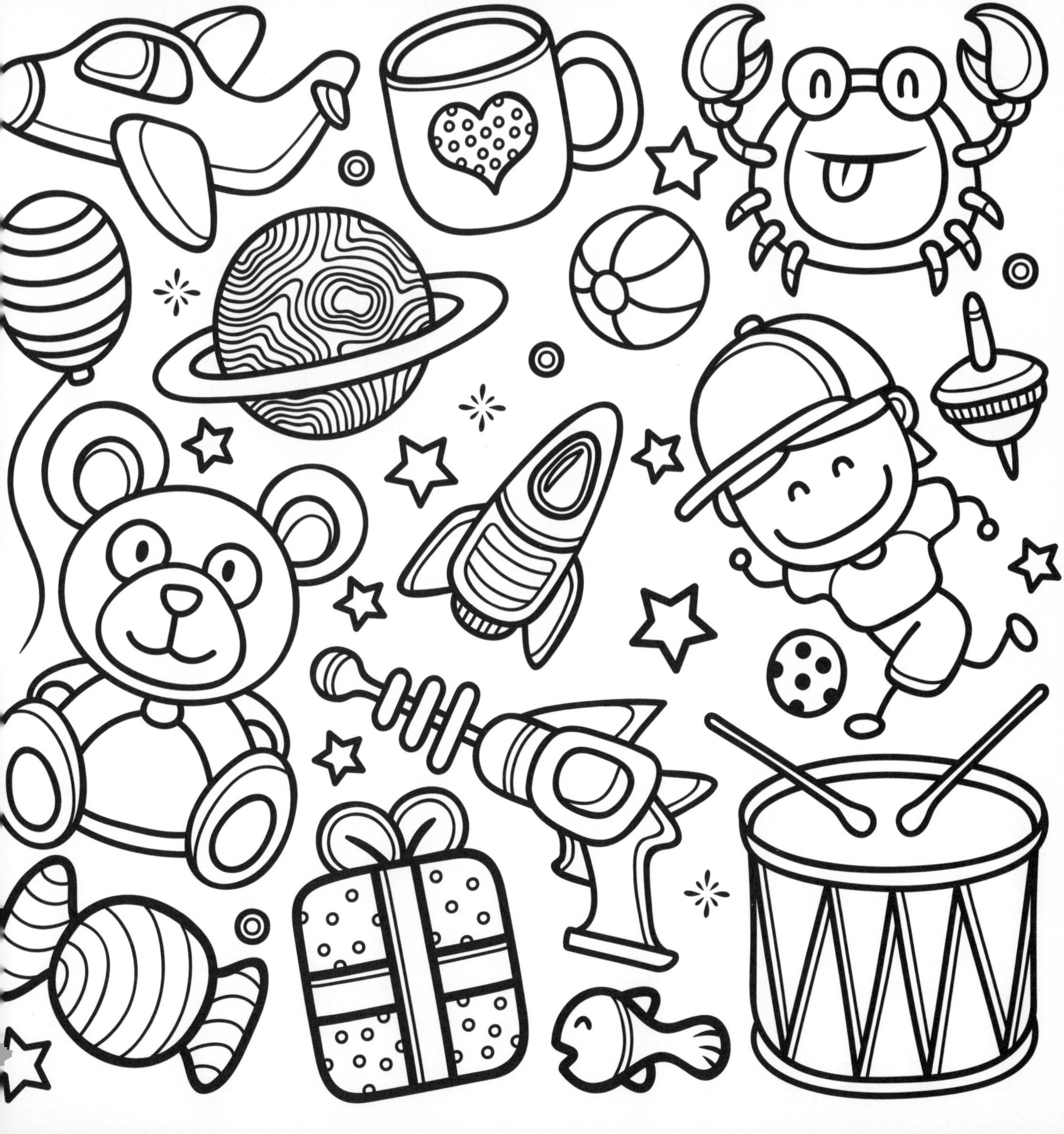

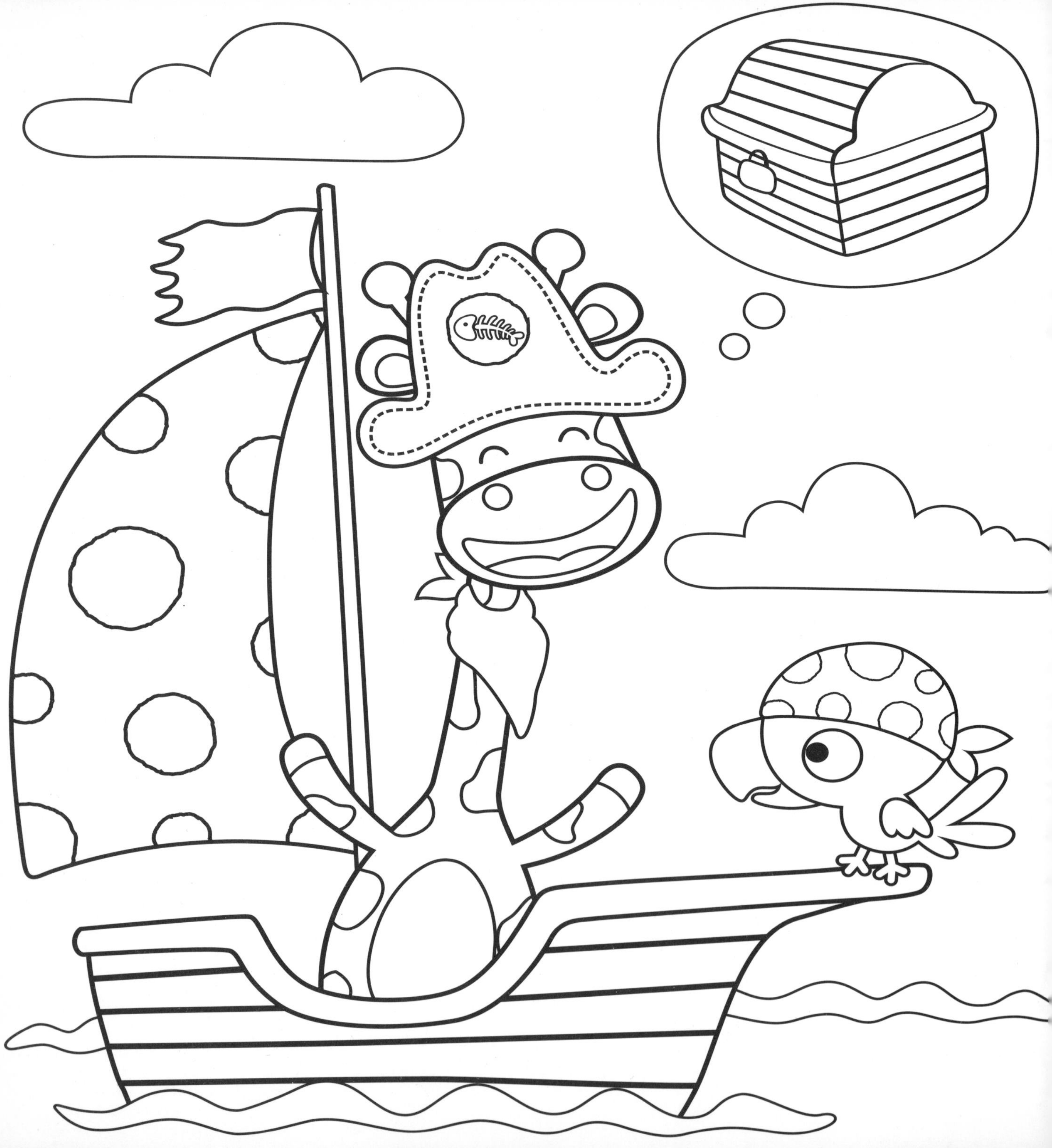

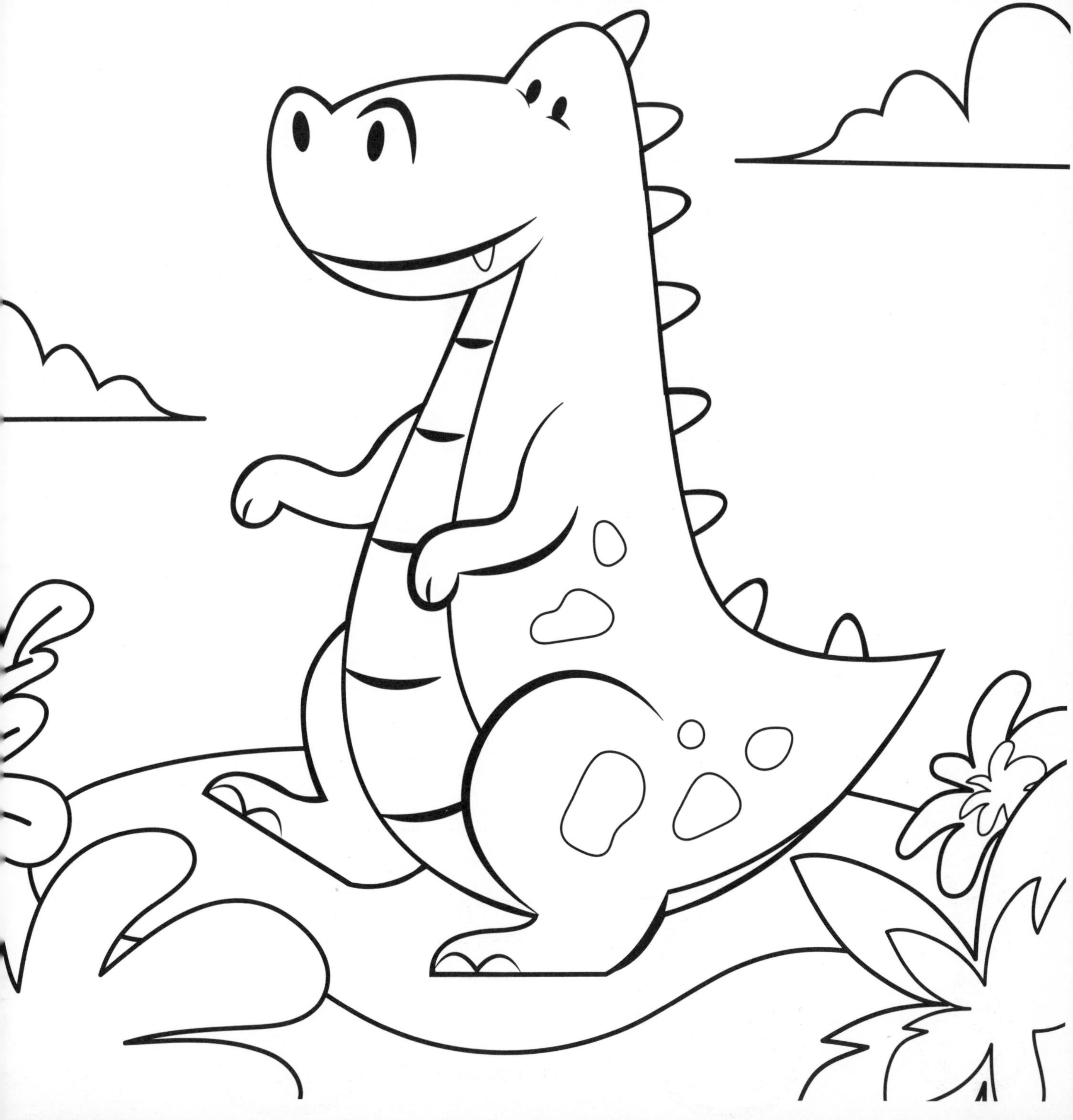

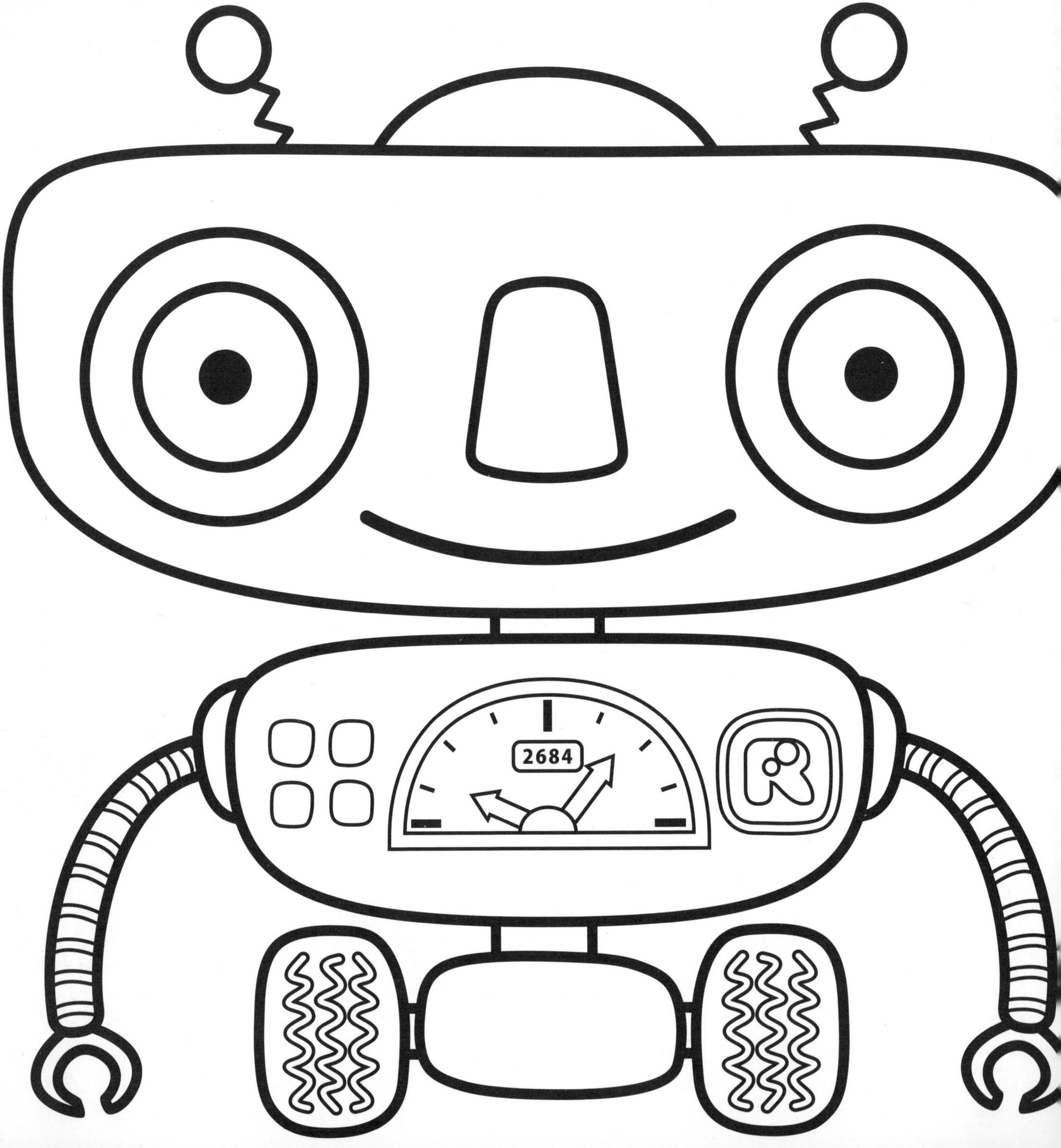
2684

TREASURE
ALL HANDS HOAY
PIRATE'S
QUEST
YO HO HO HO

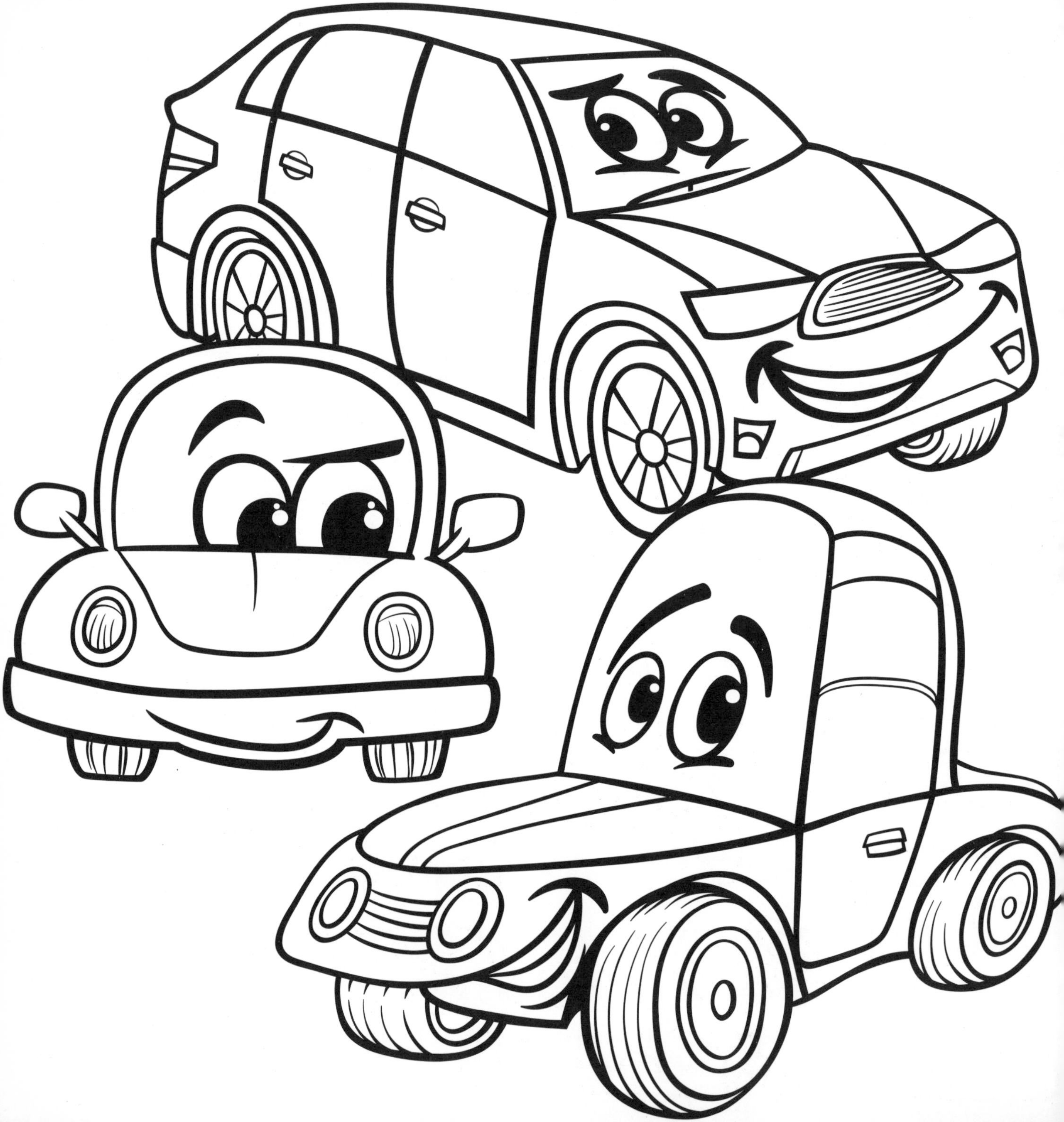

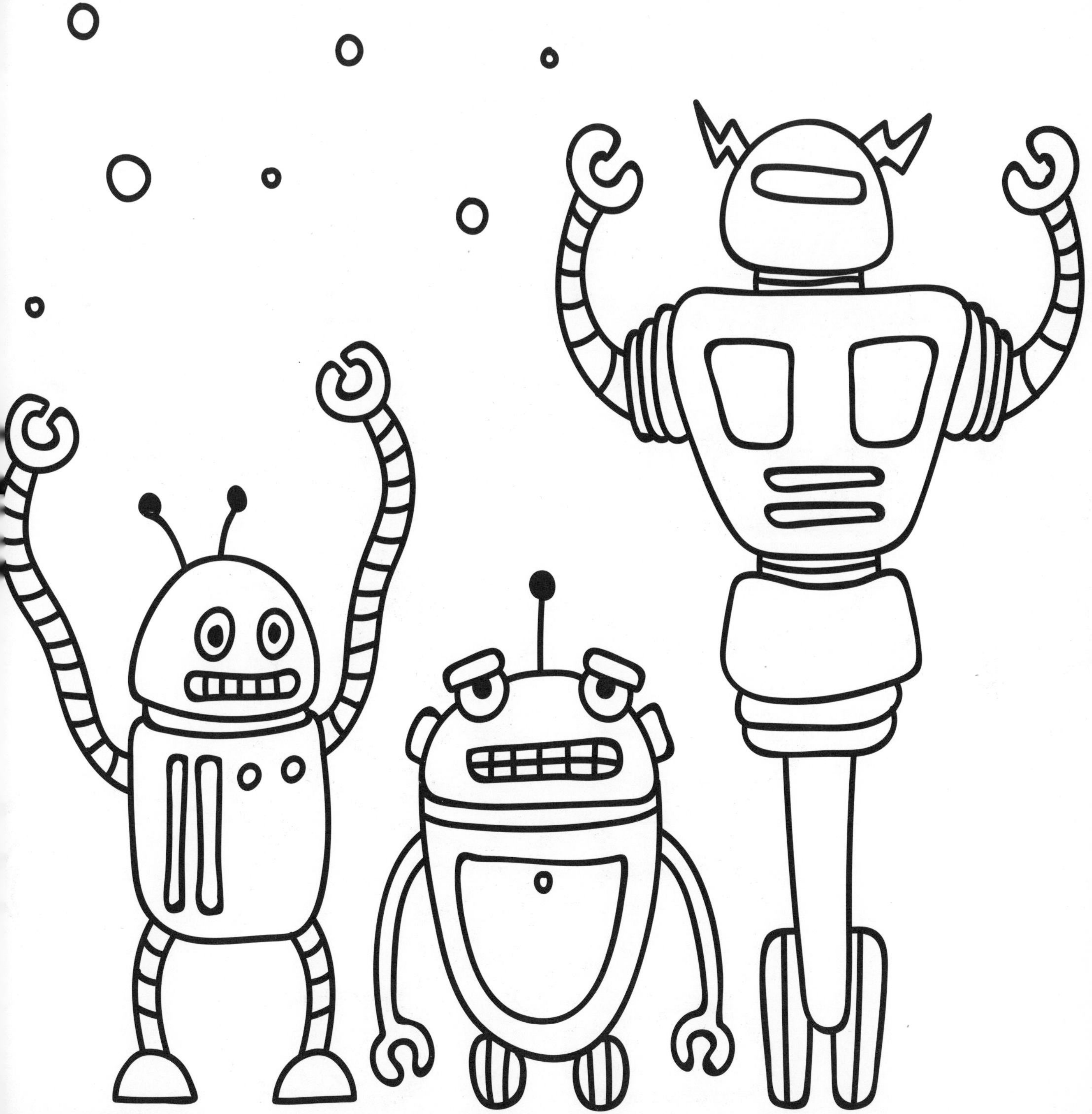

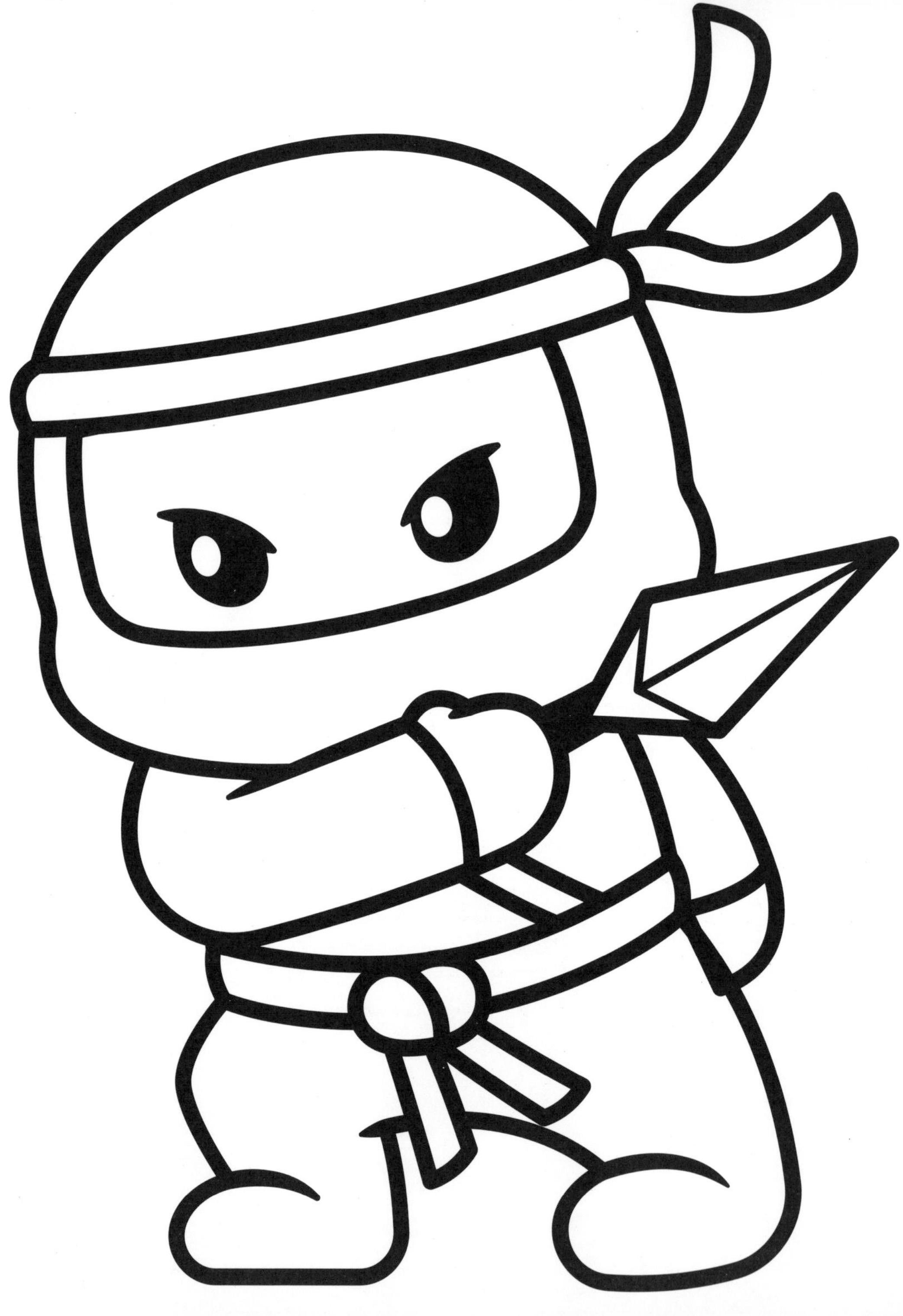

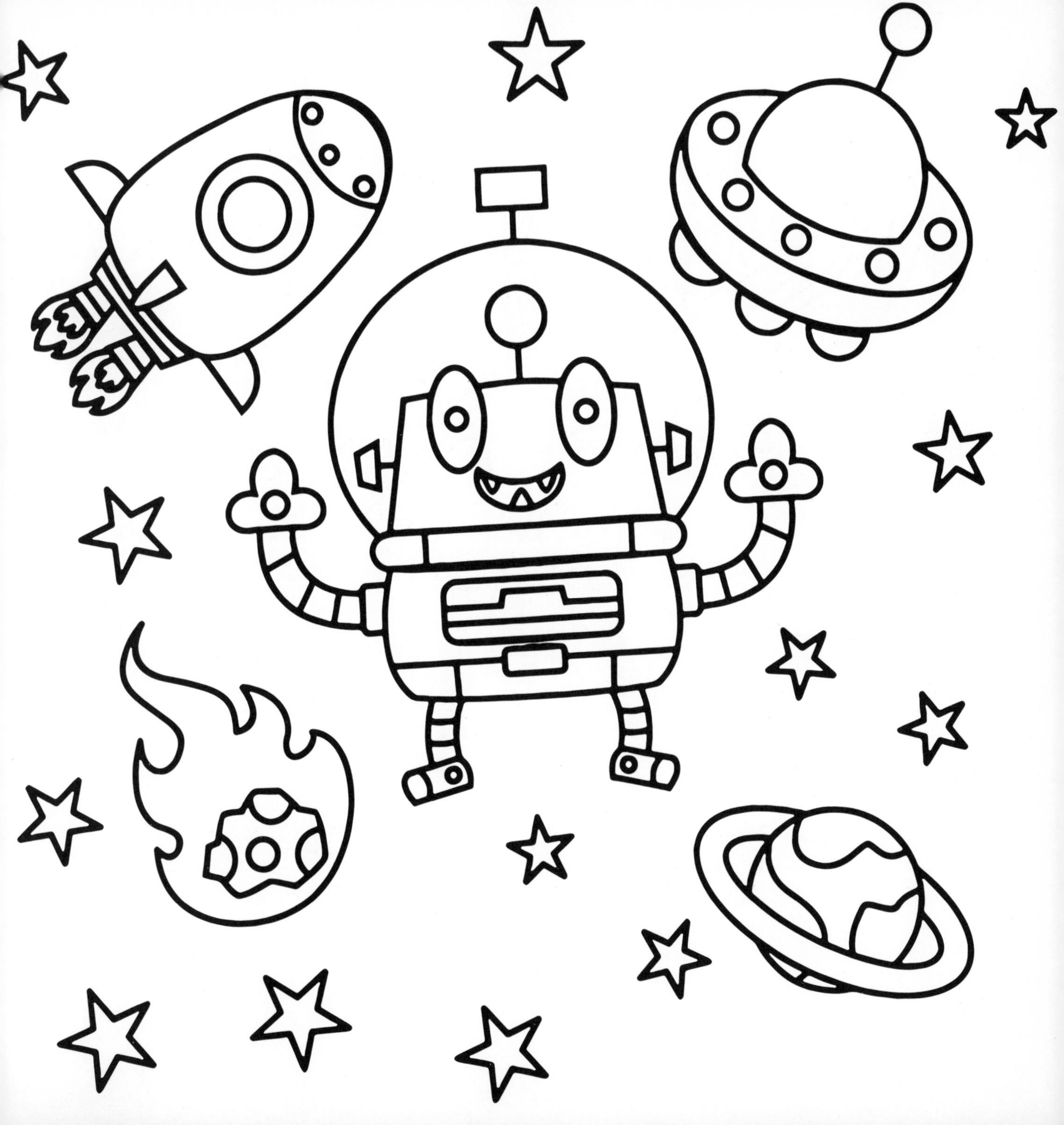

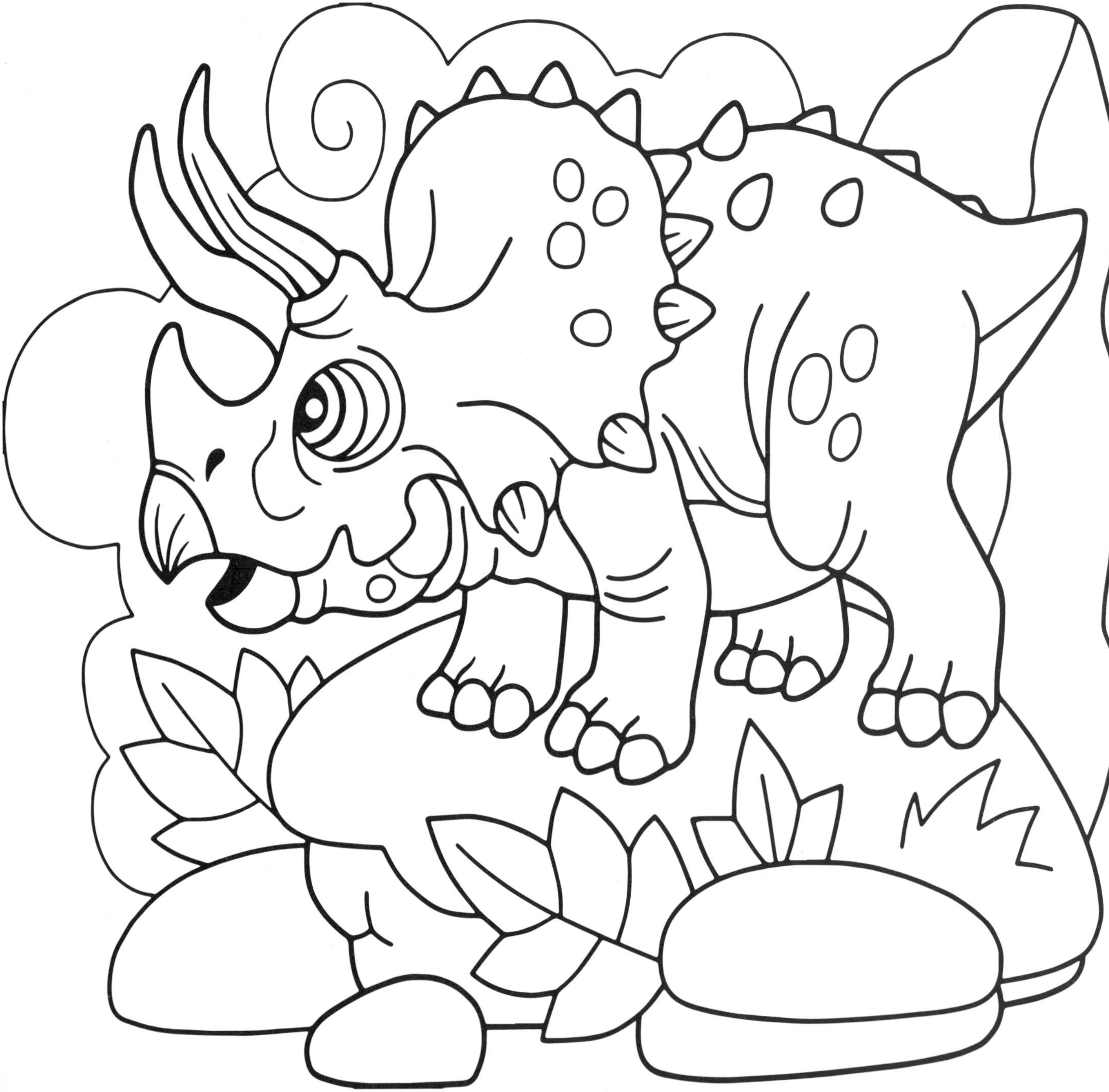

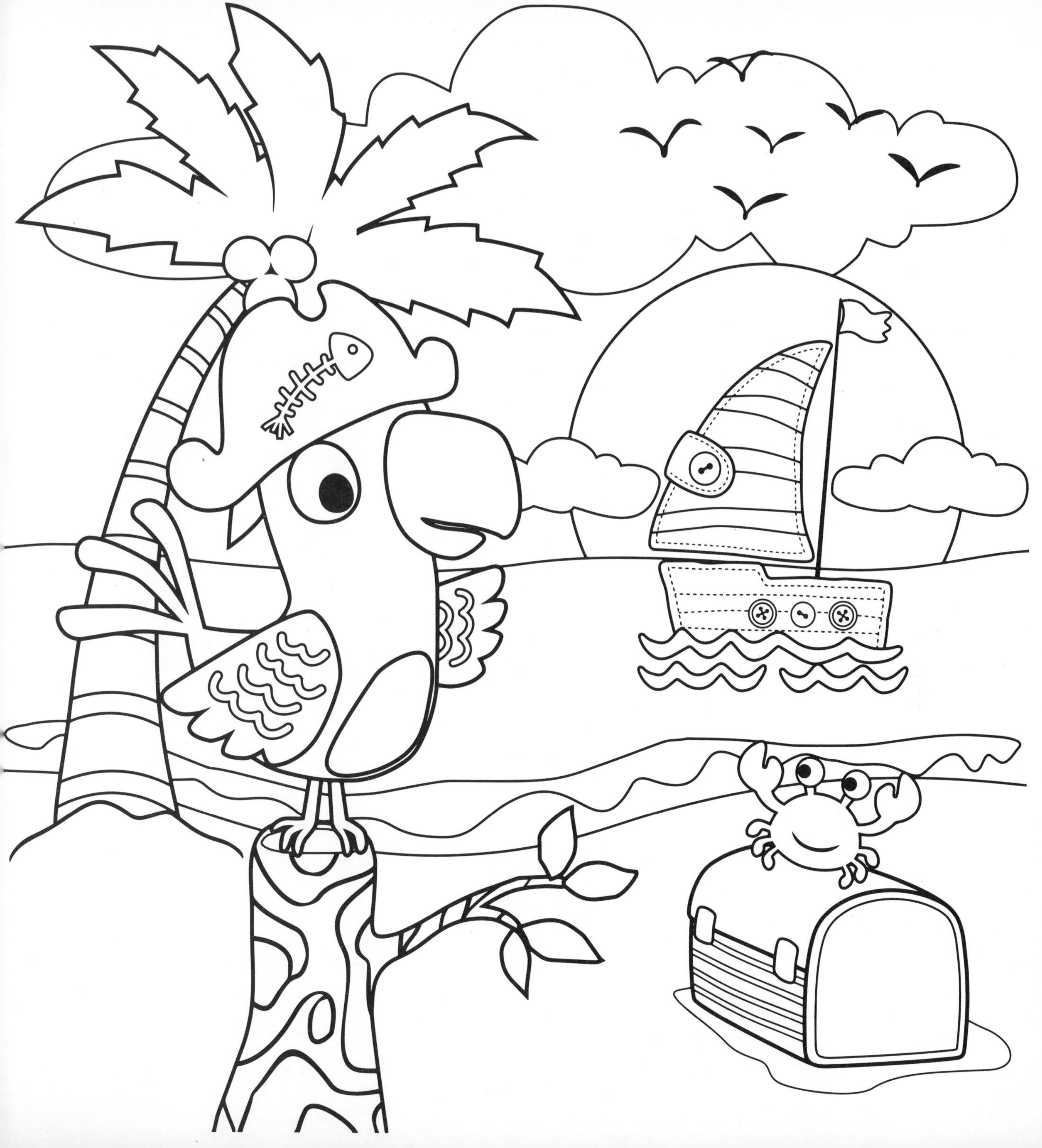

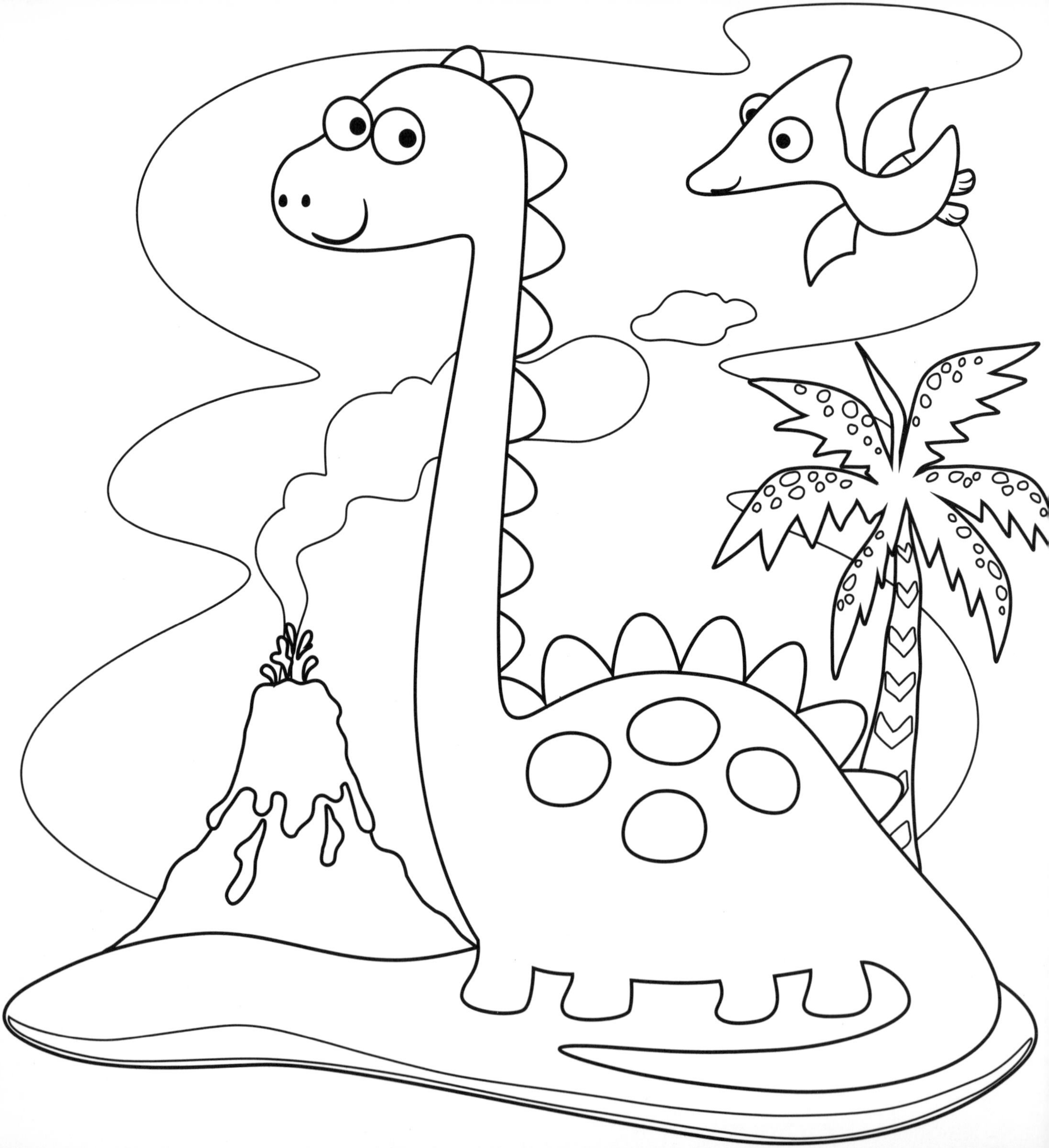

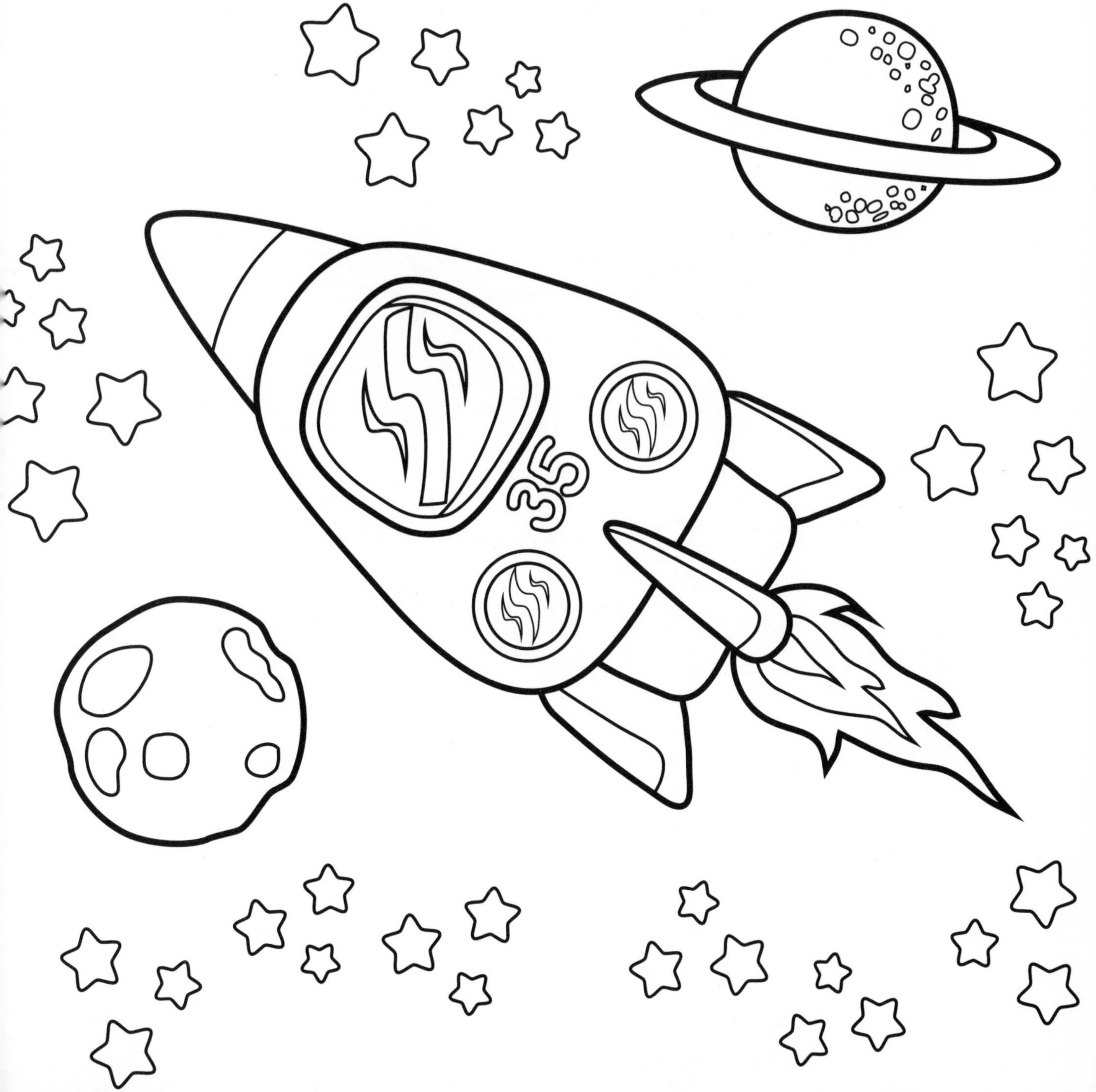
35

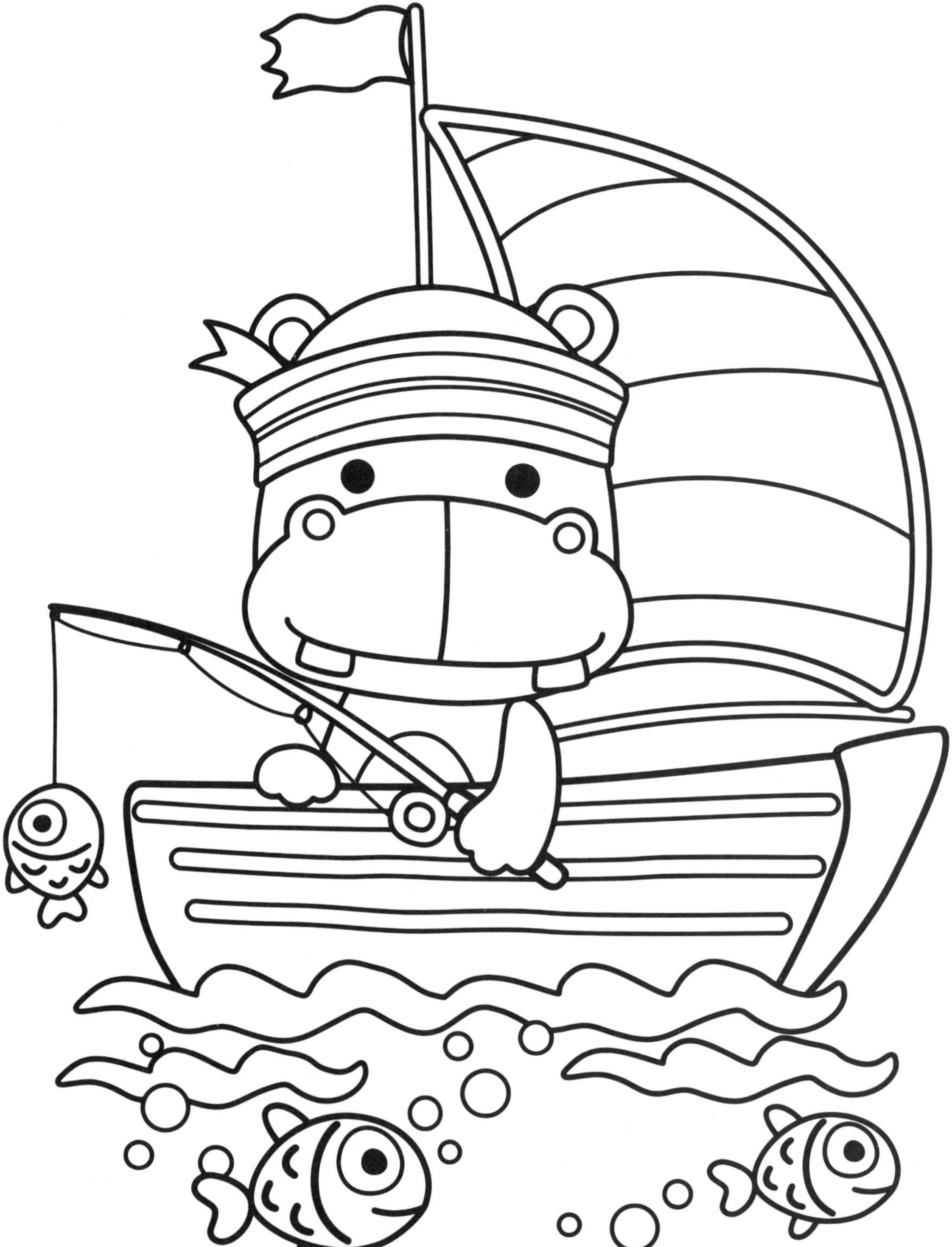

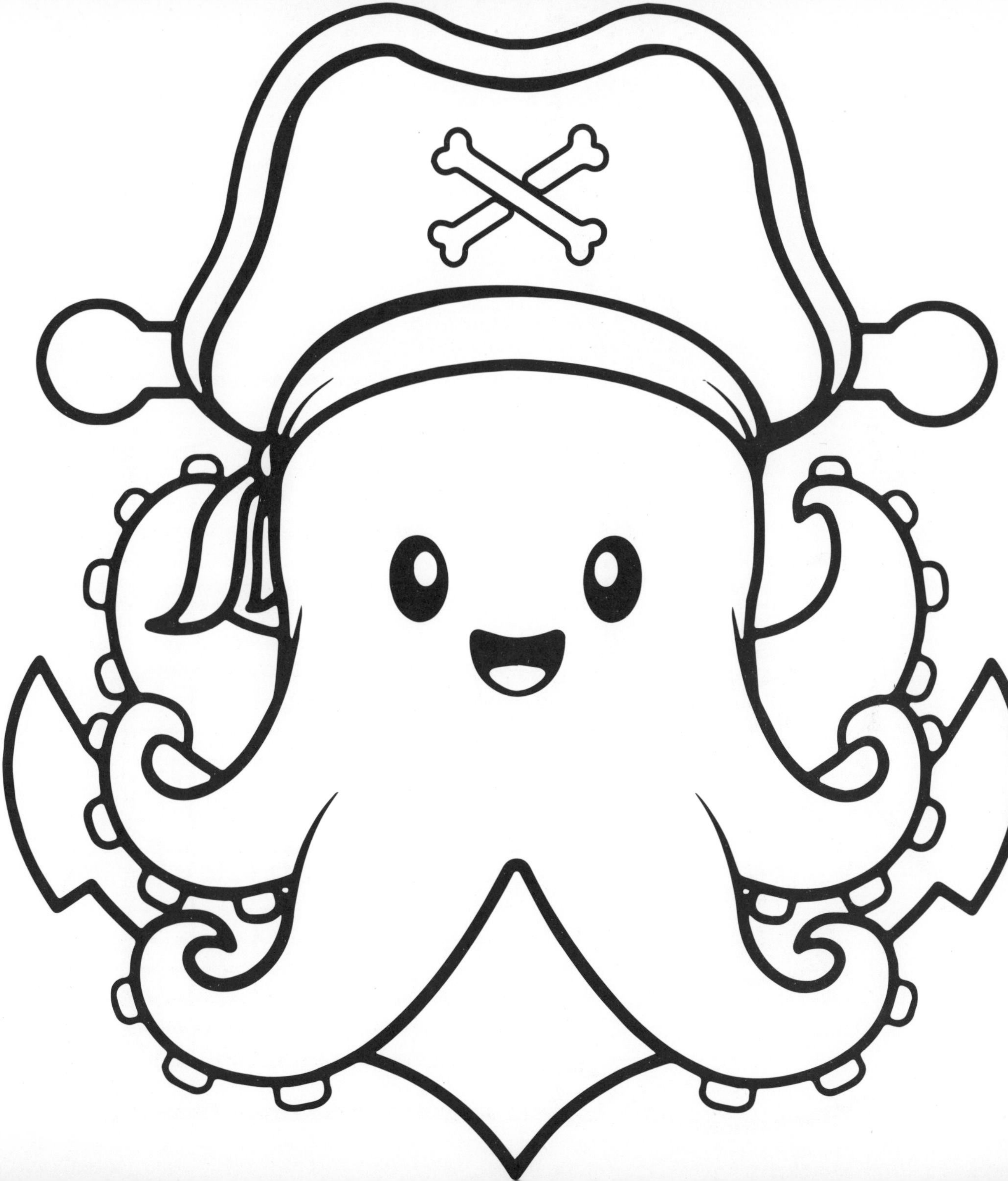

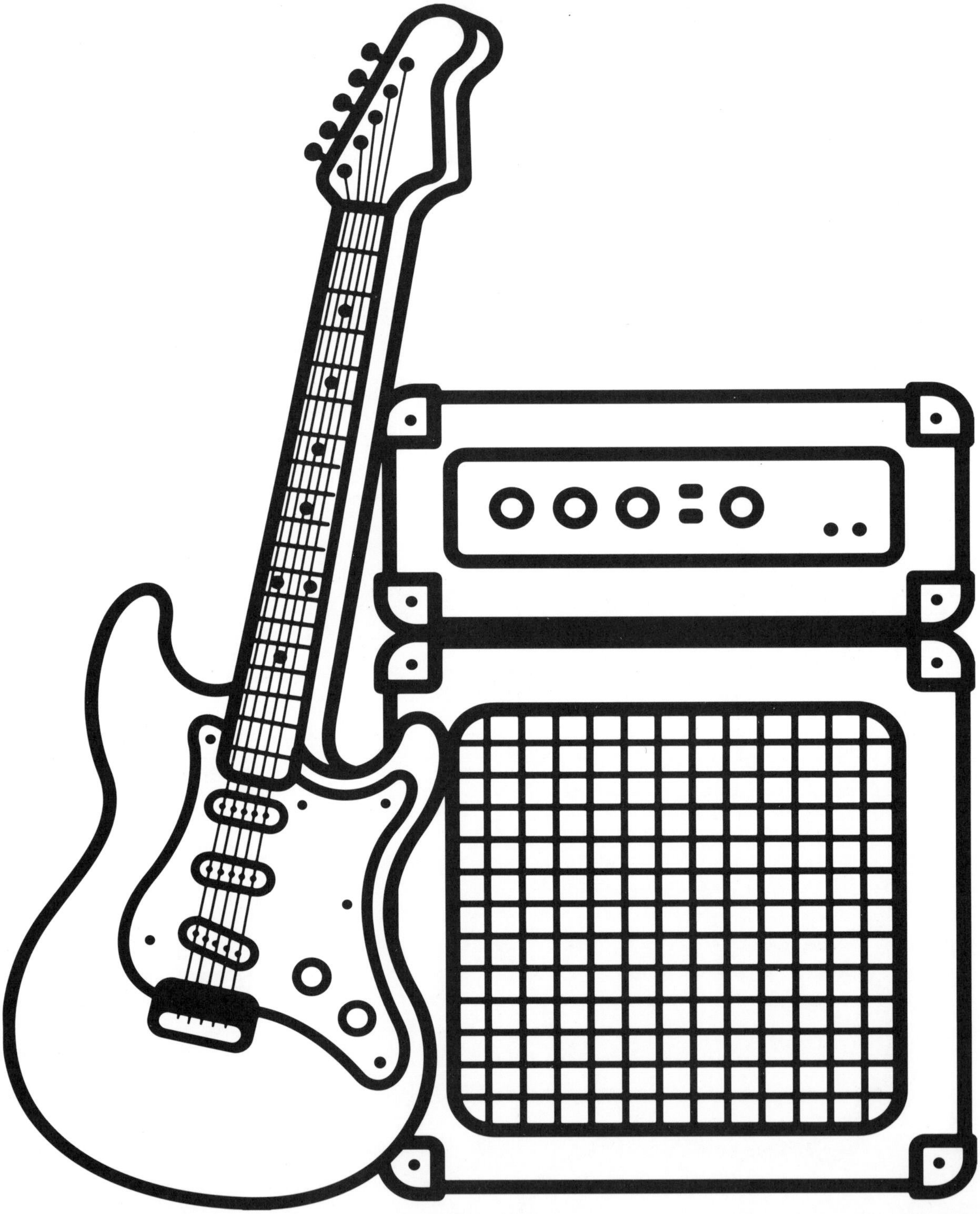

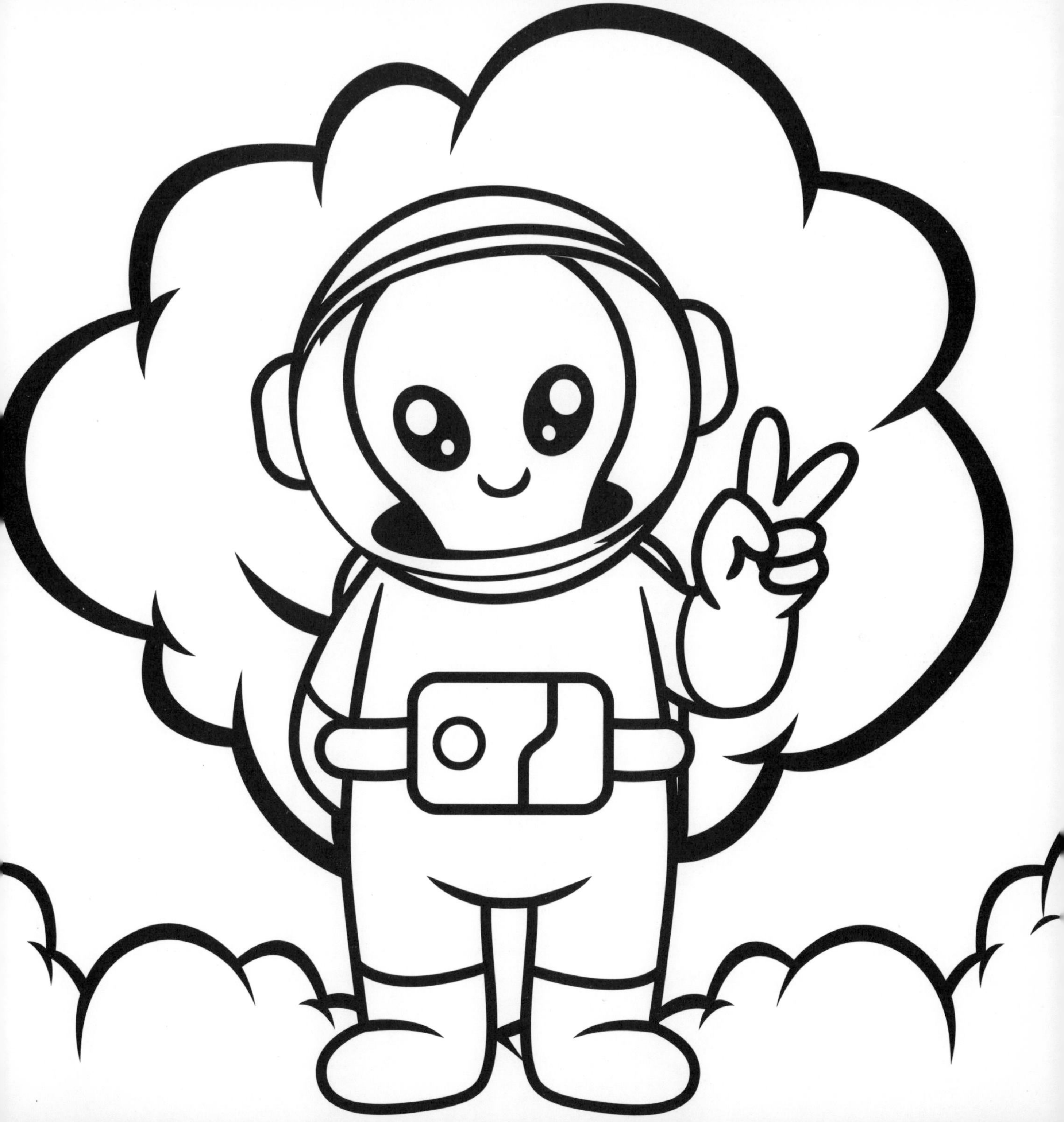

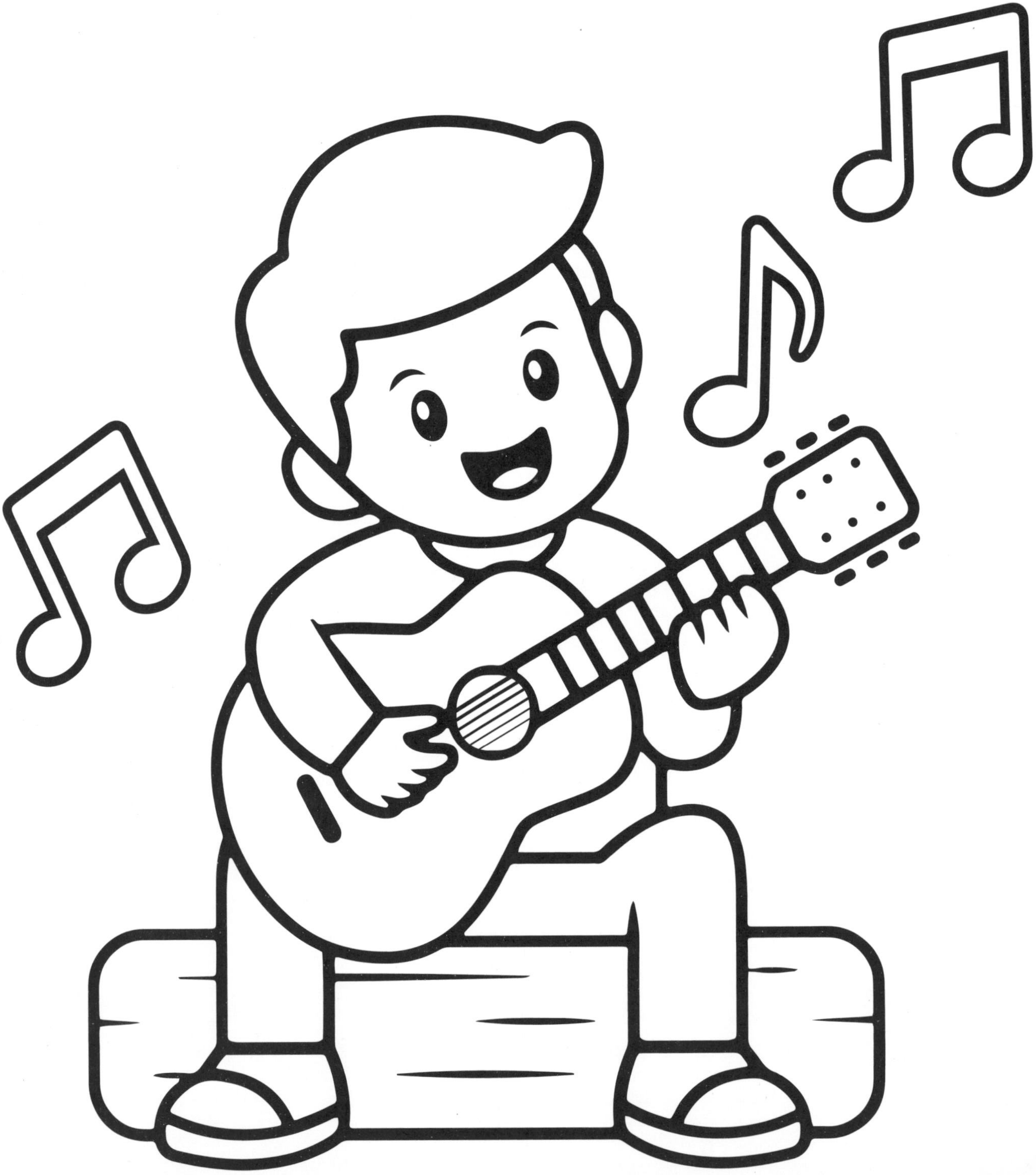

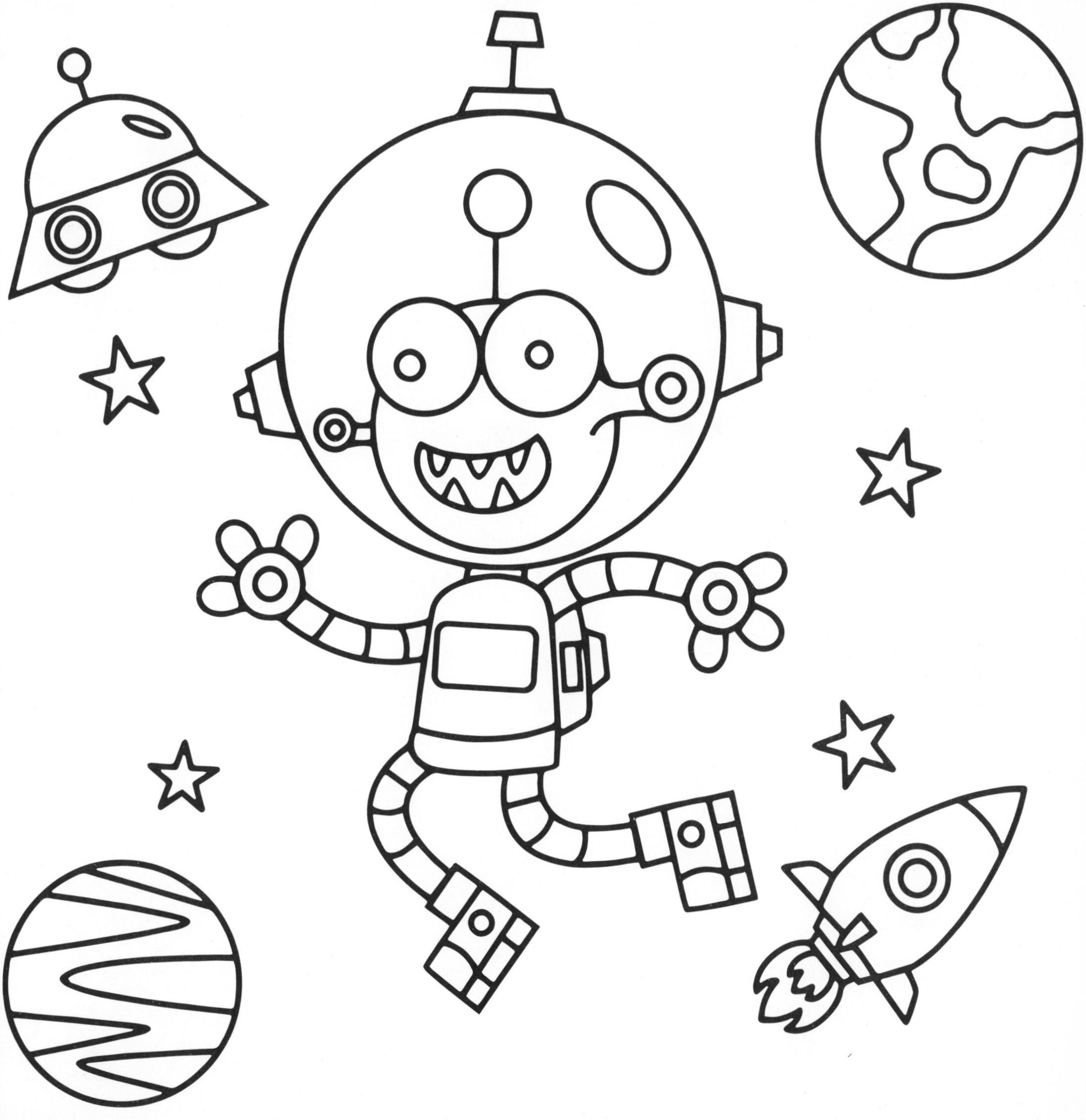

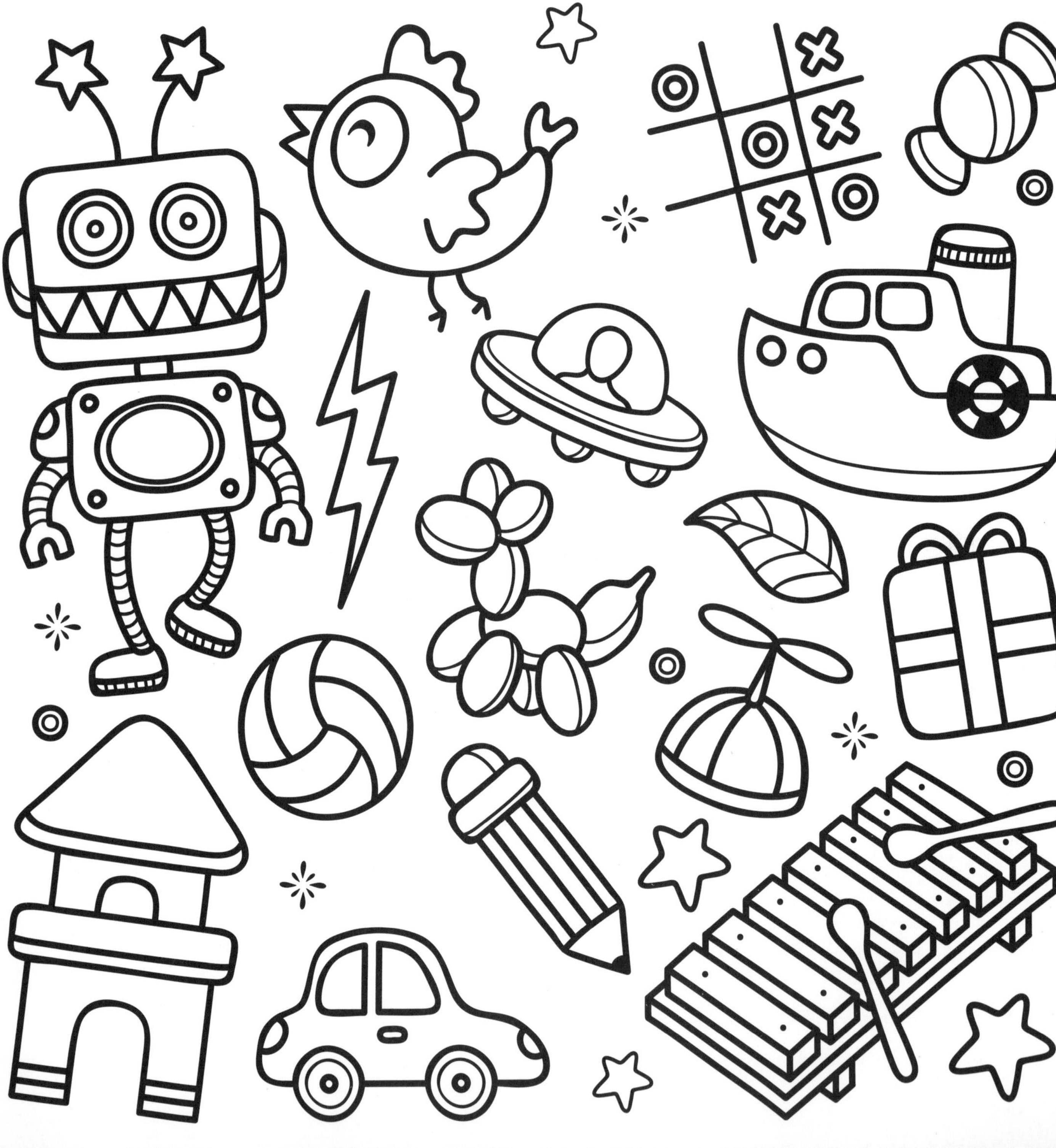

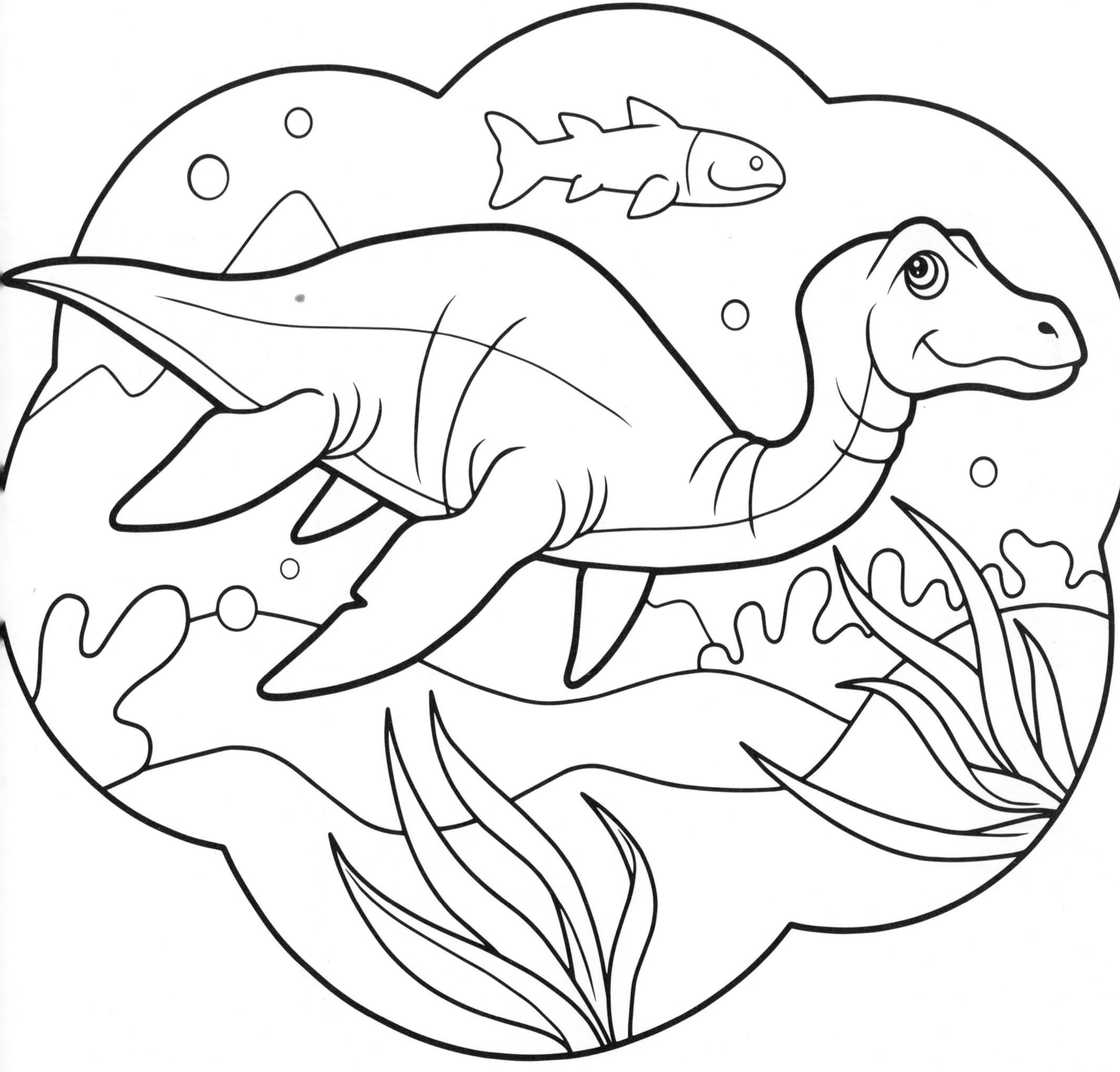

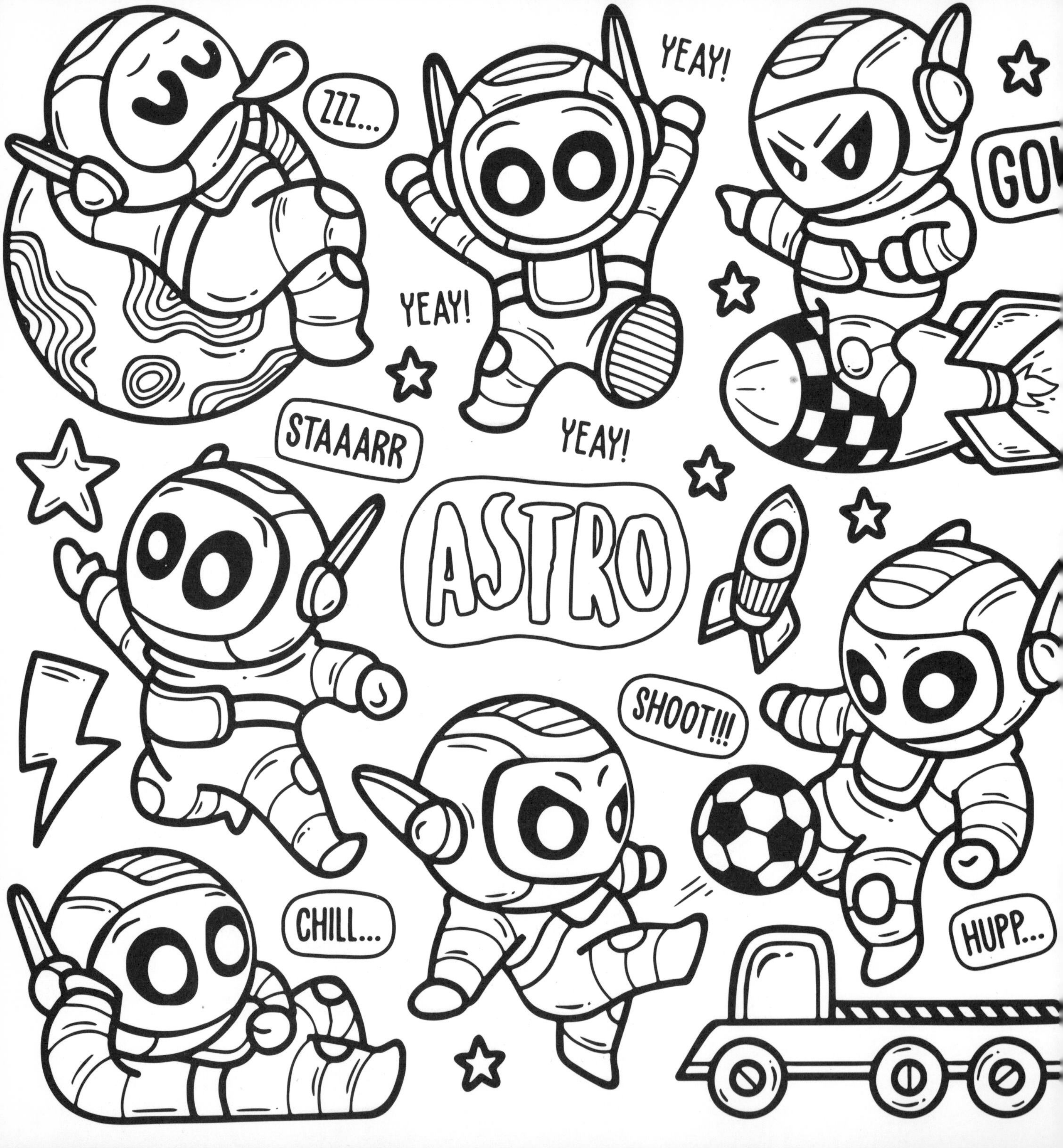
ZZZ...
YEAY!
GO
YEAY!
STAAARR
YEAY!
ASTRO
SHOOT!!!
CHILL...
HUPP...

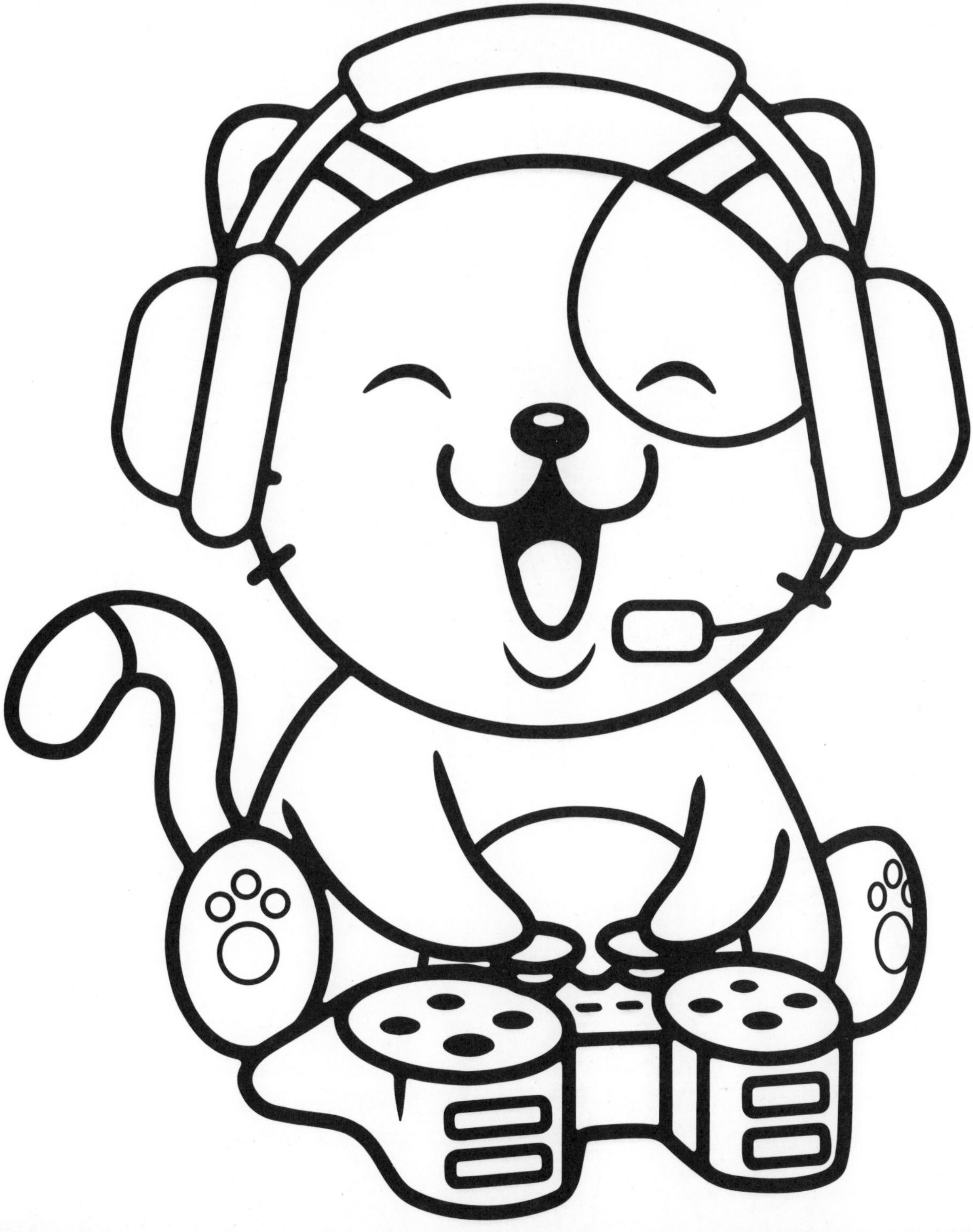

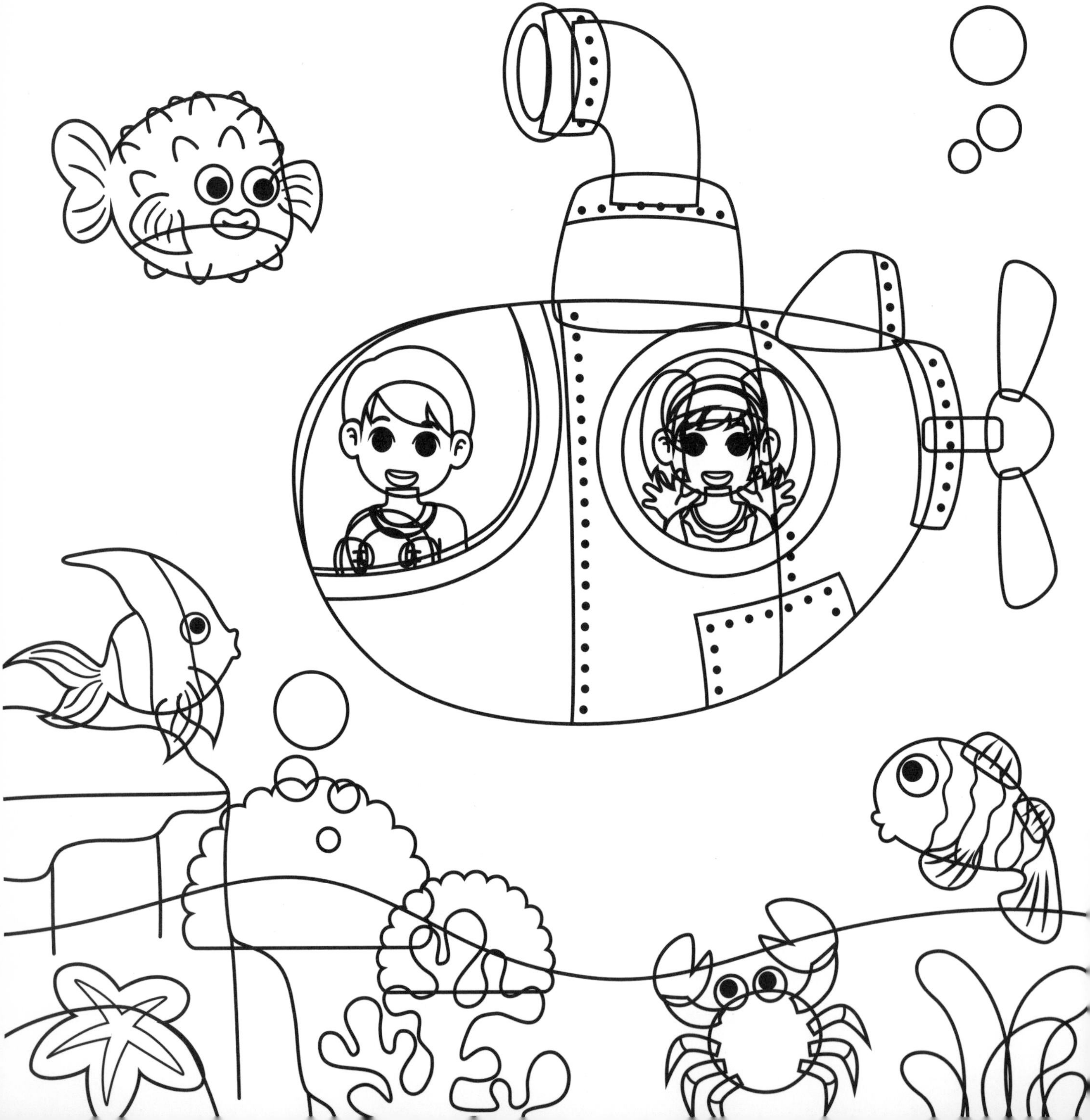

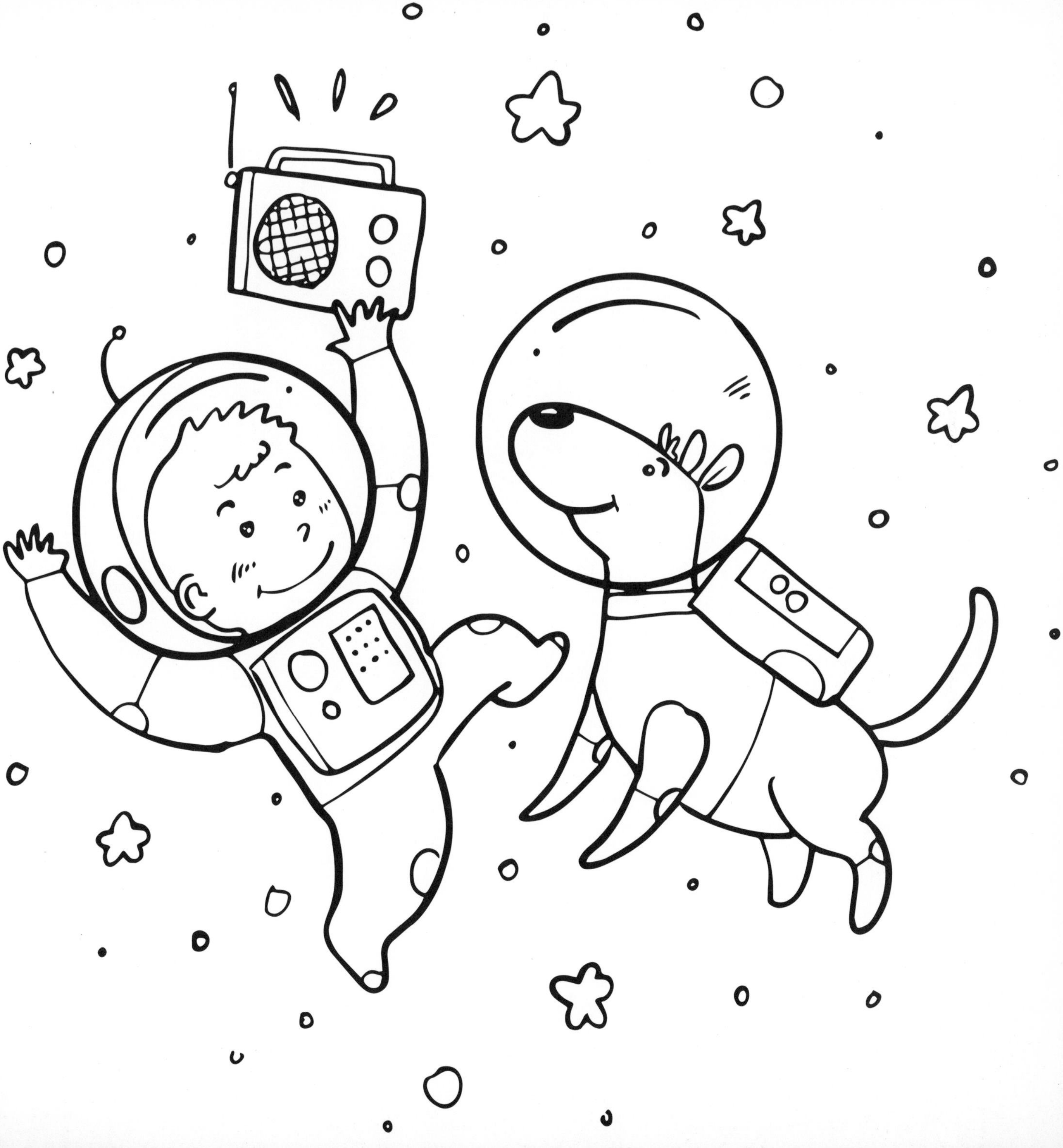

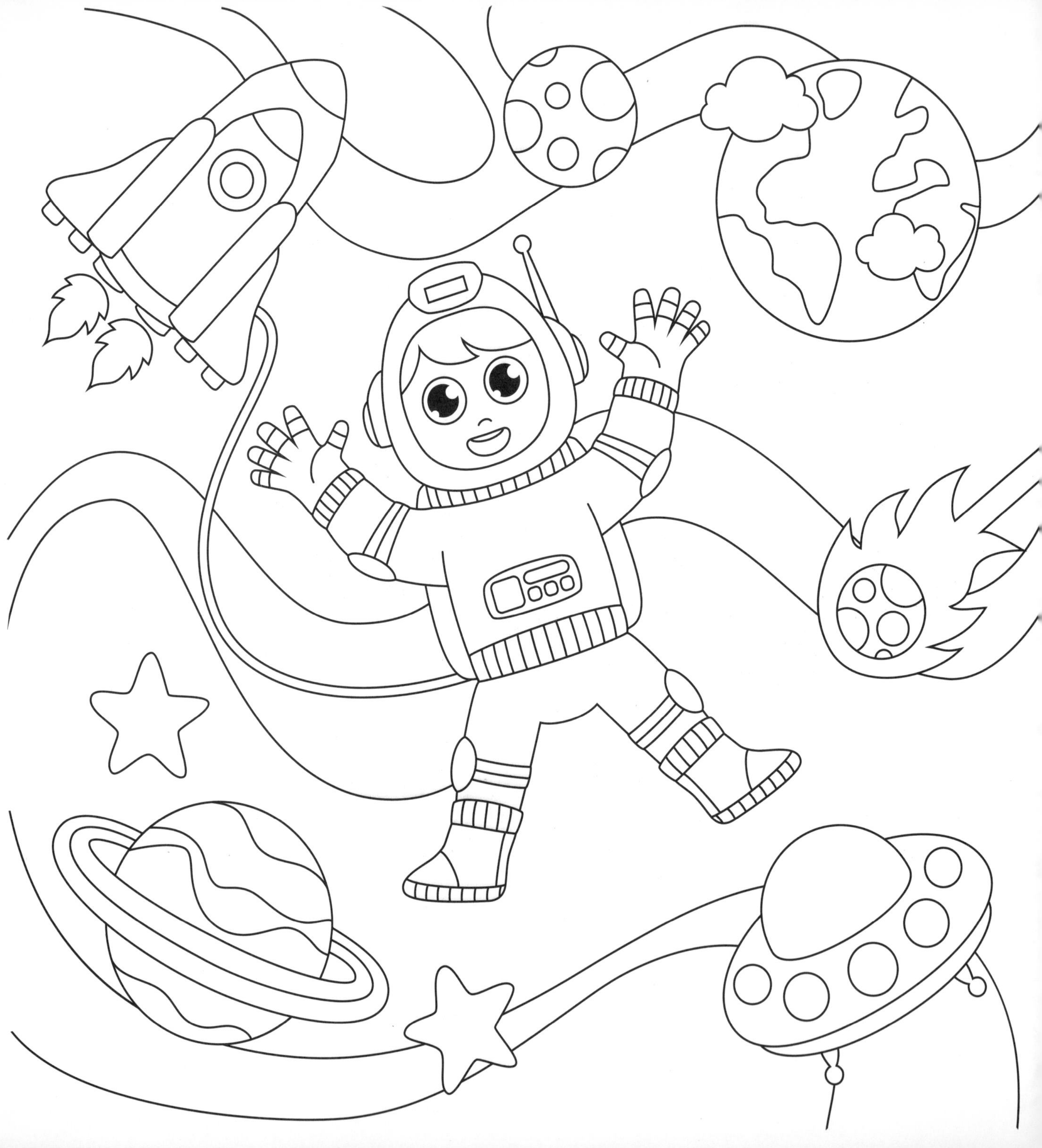

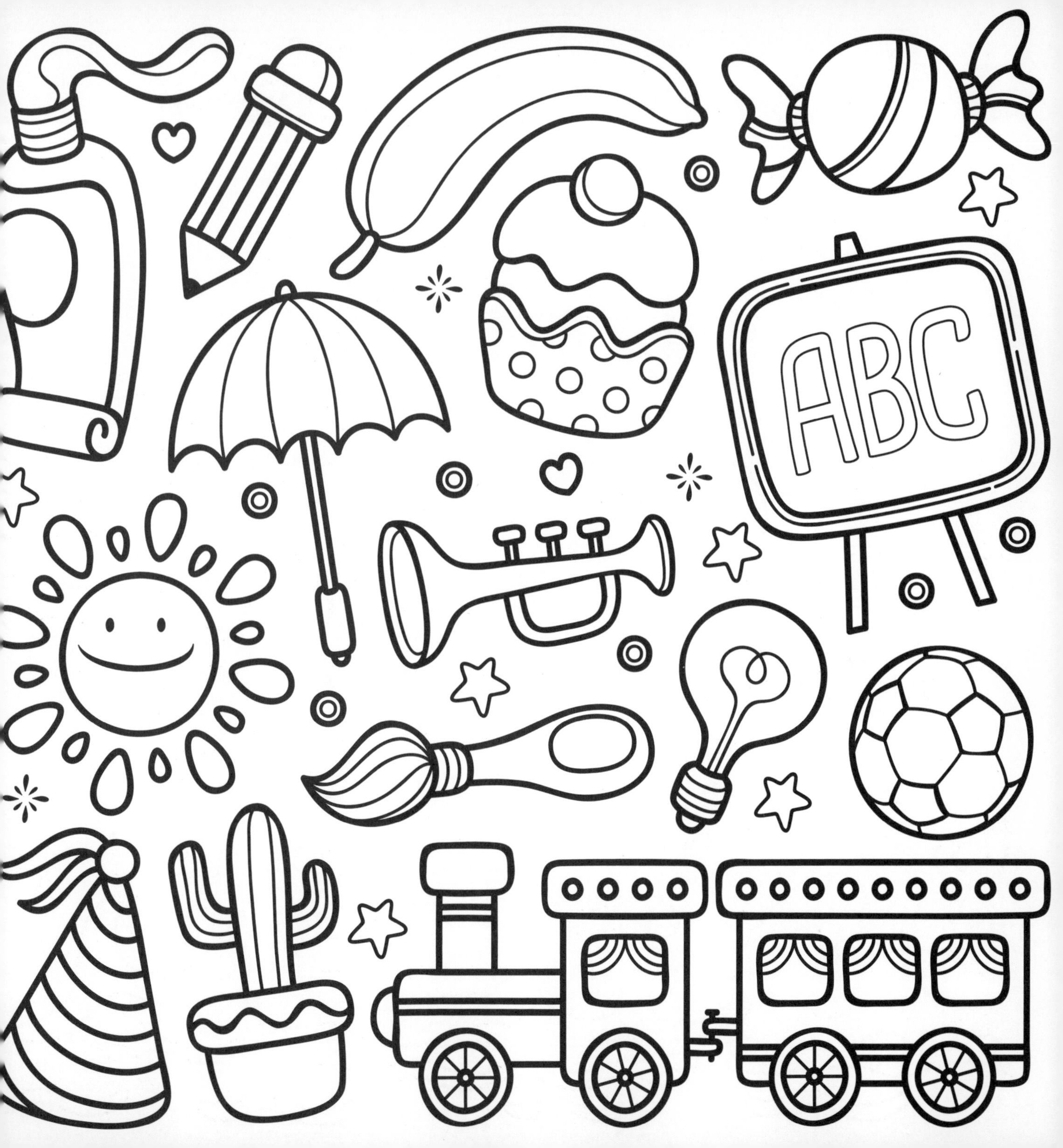
ABC

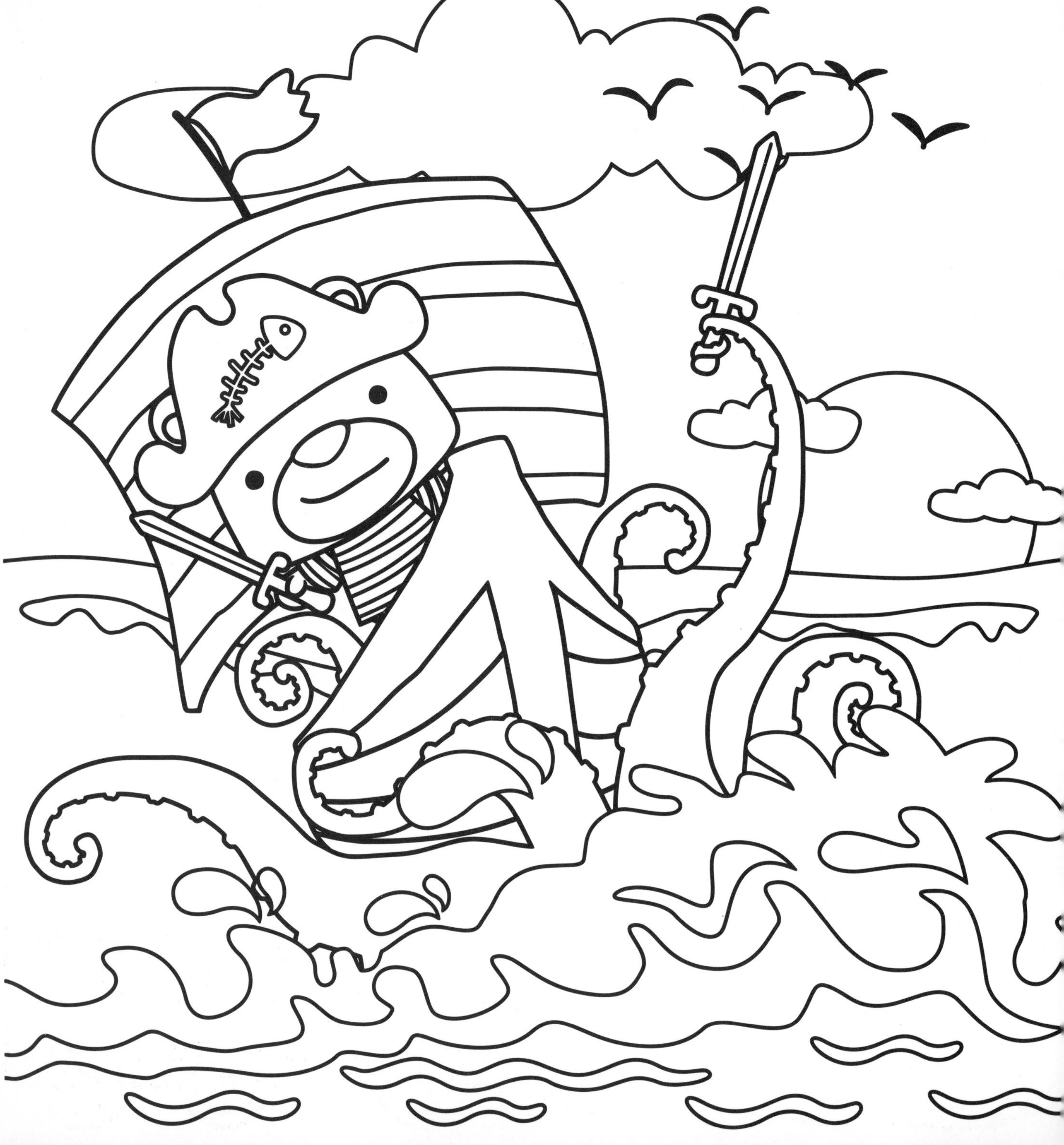

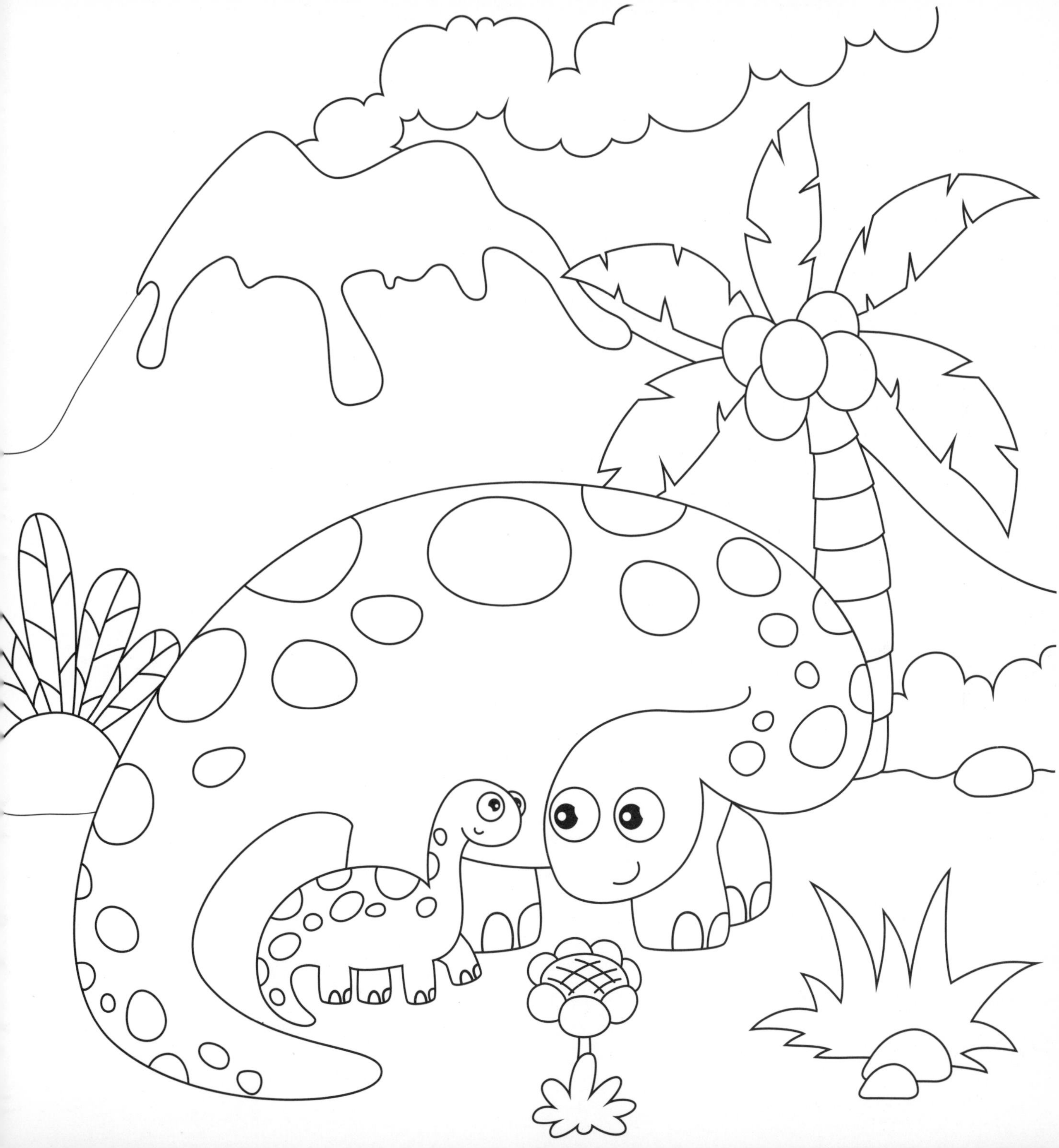

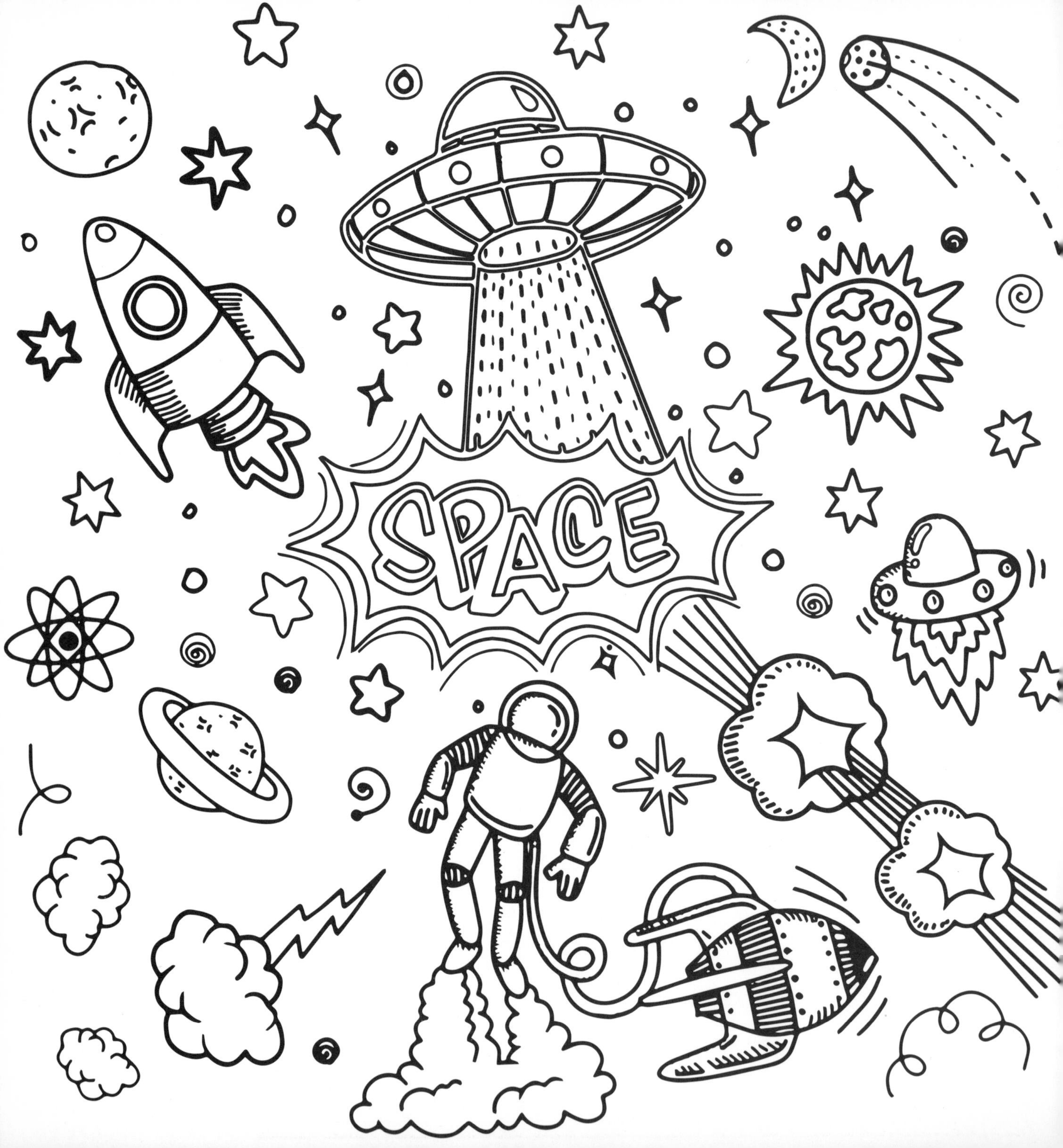
SPACE

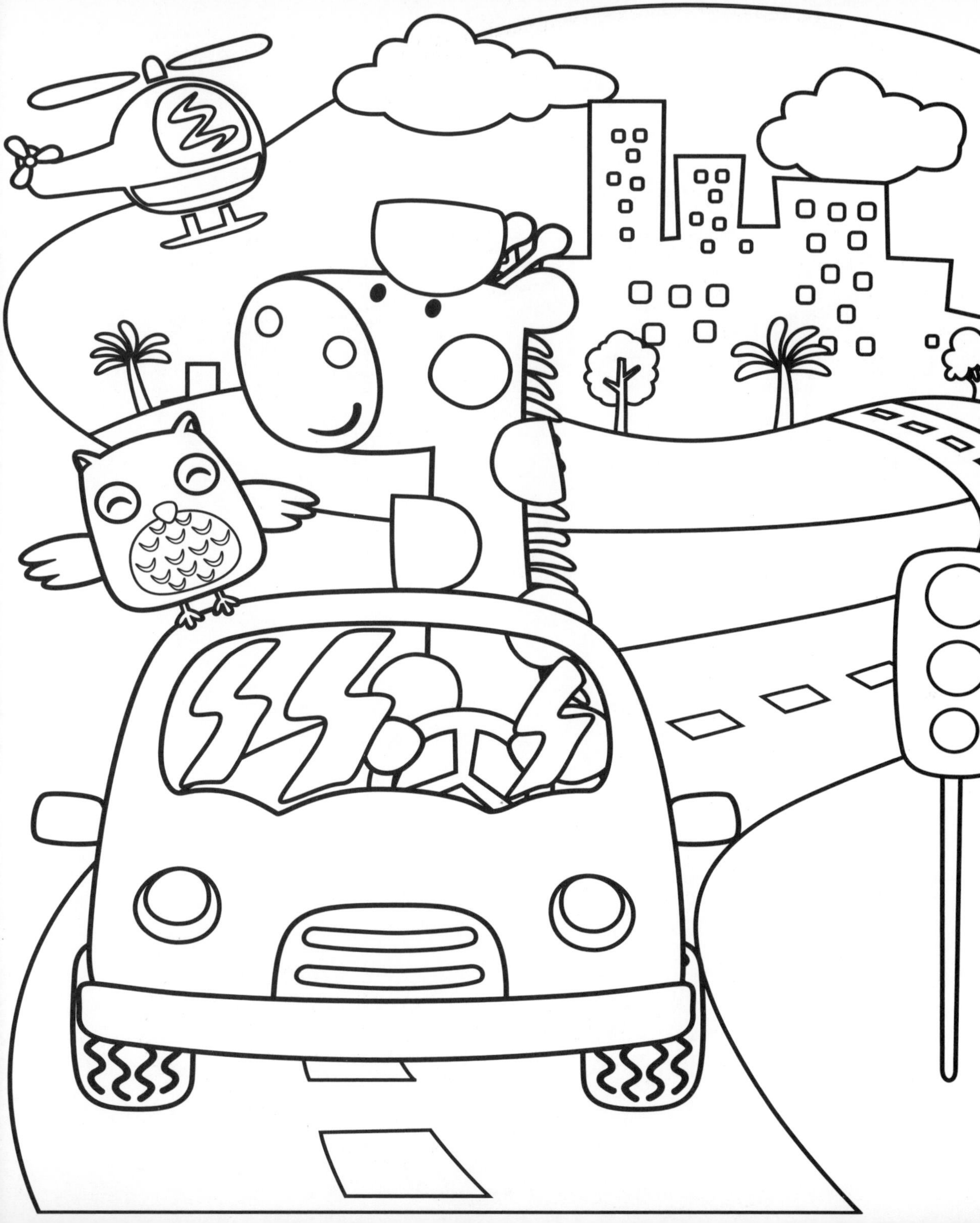

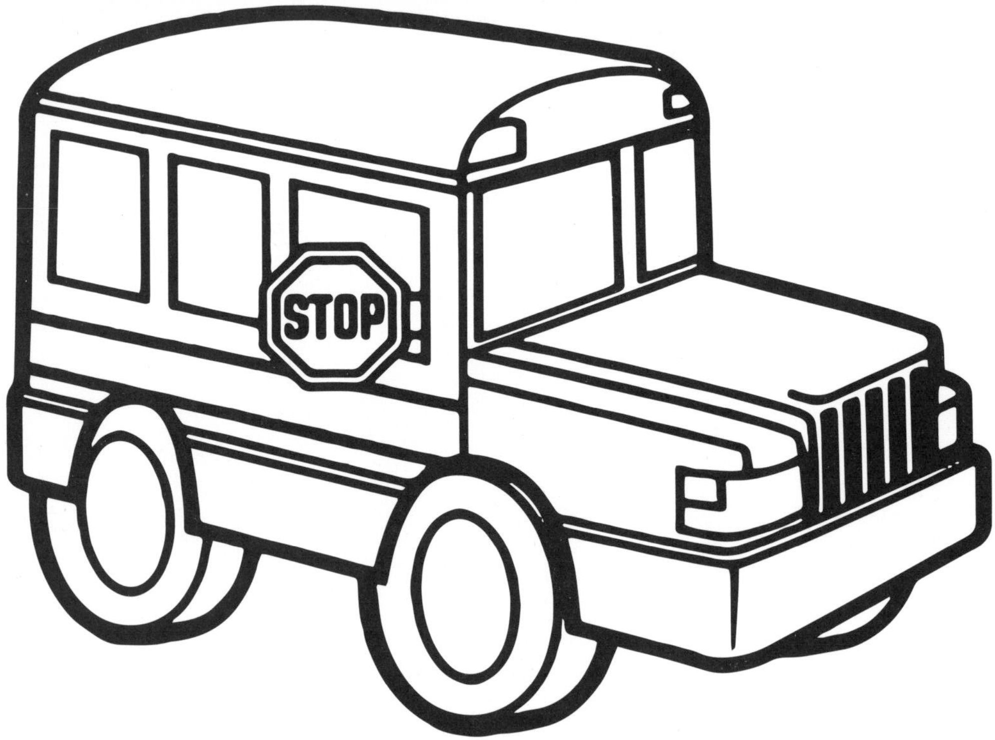
STOP

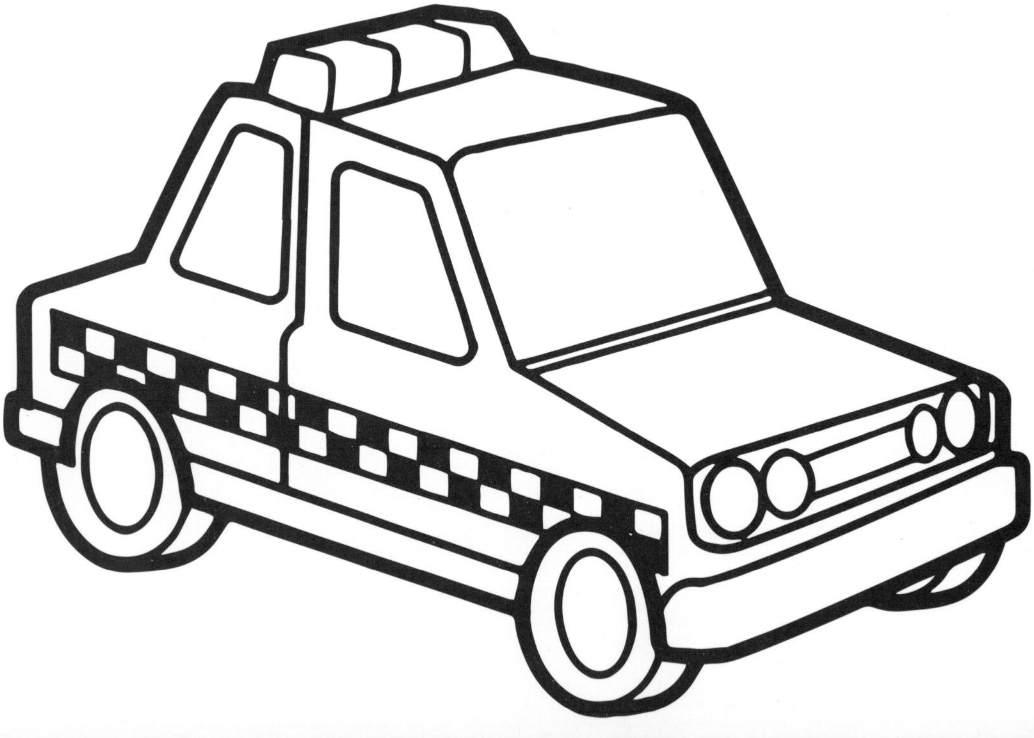

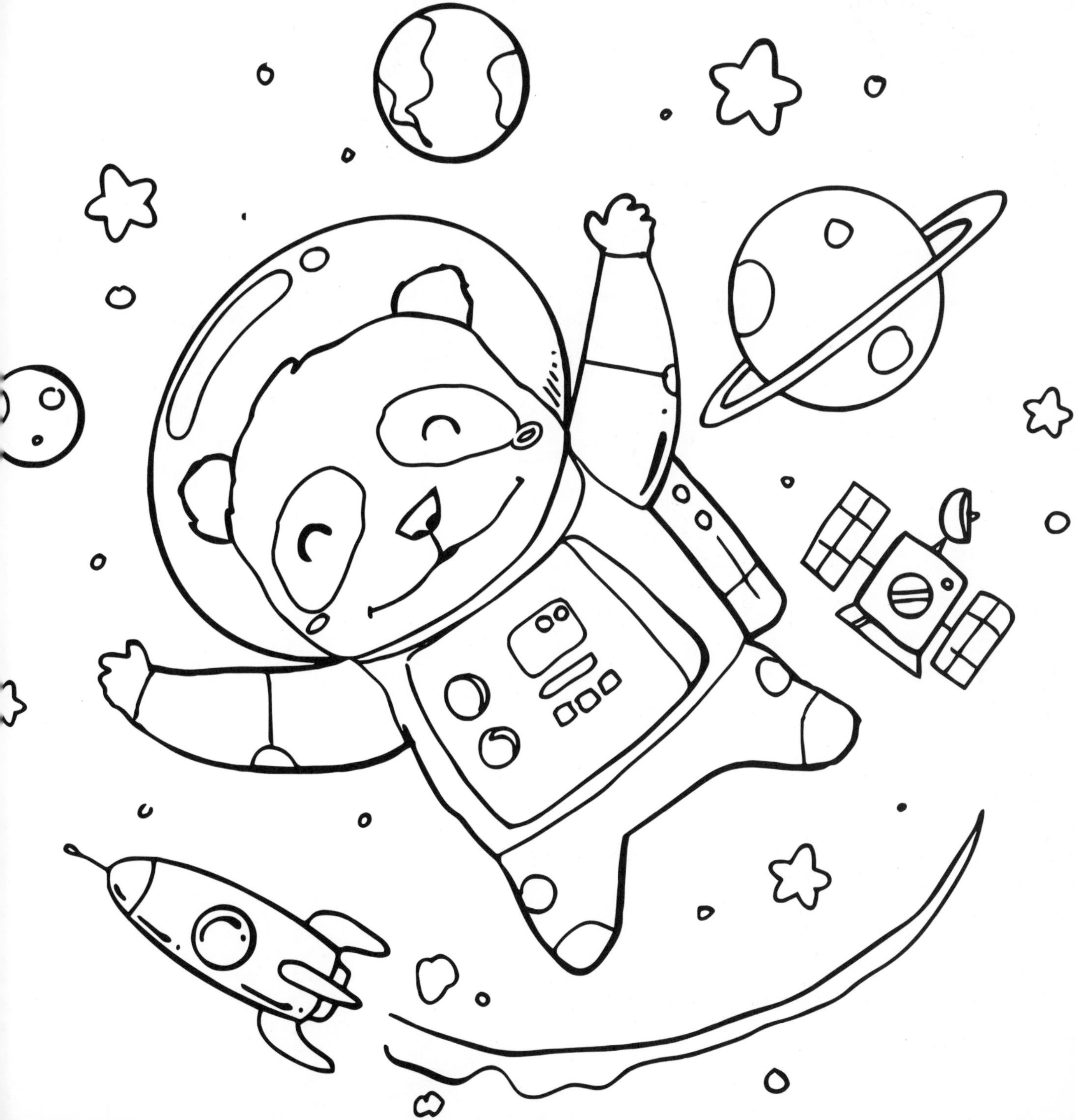

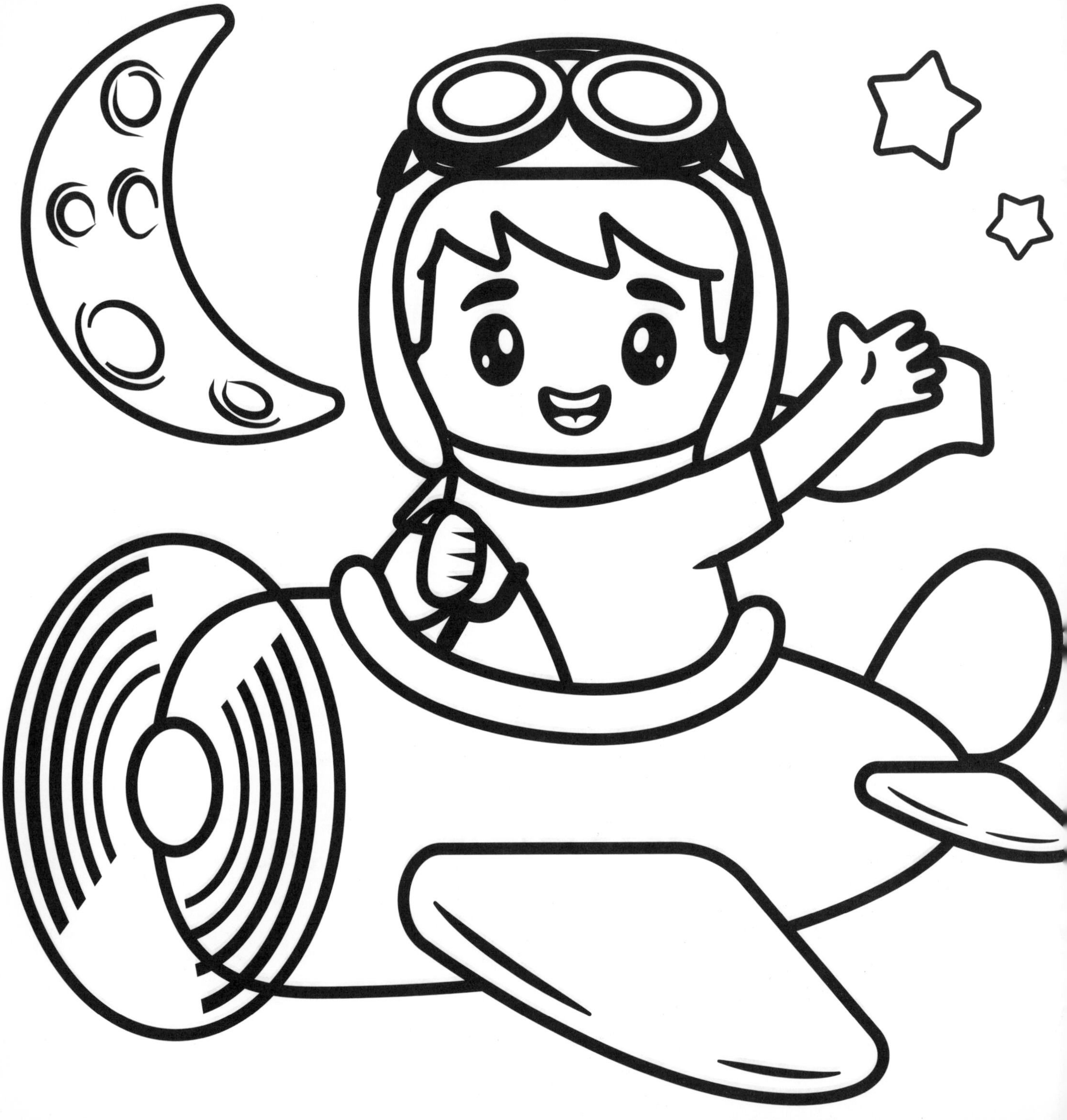

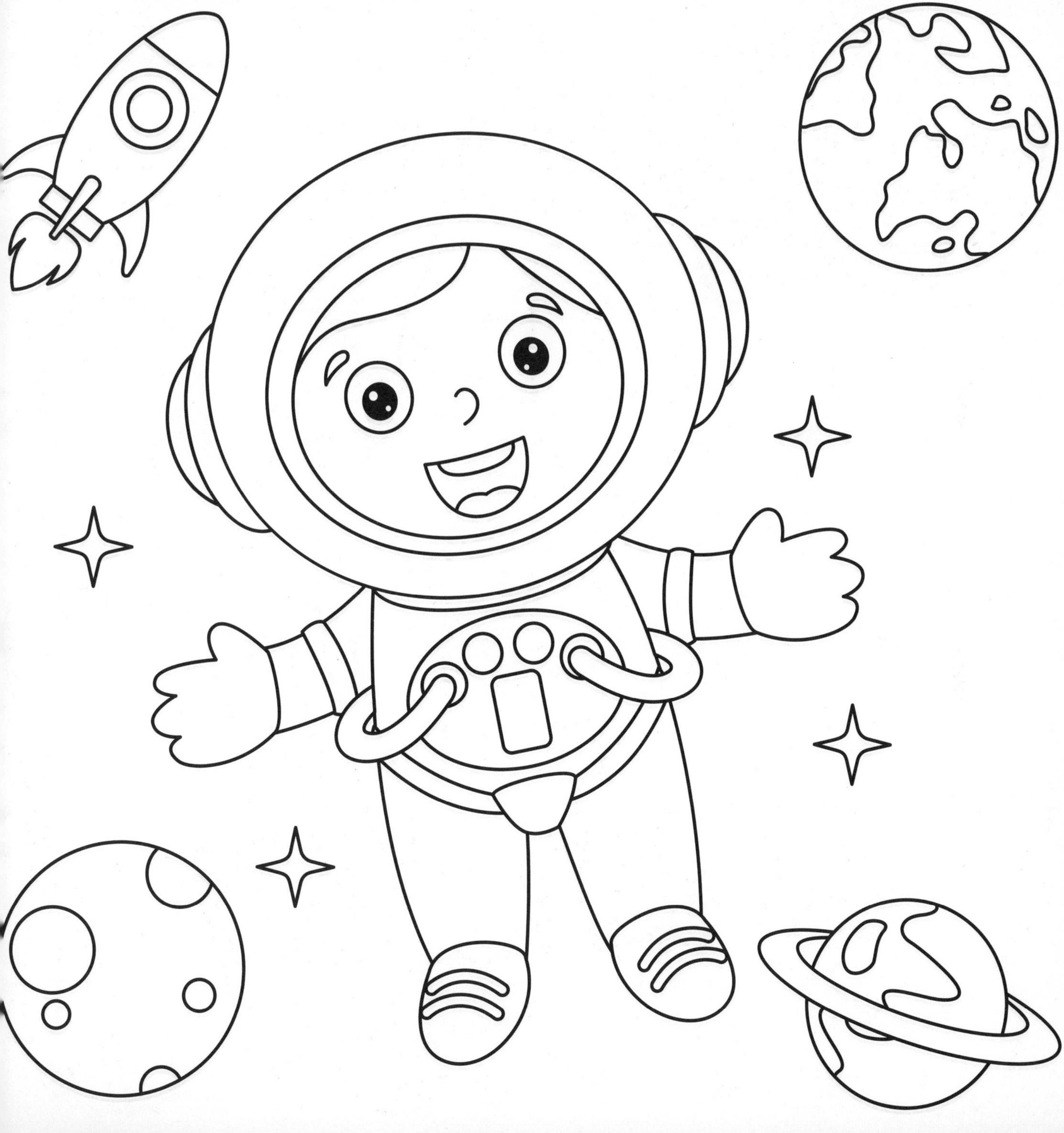

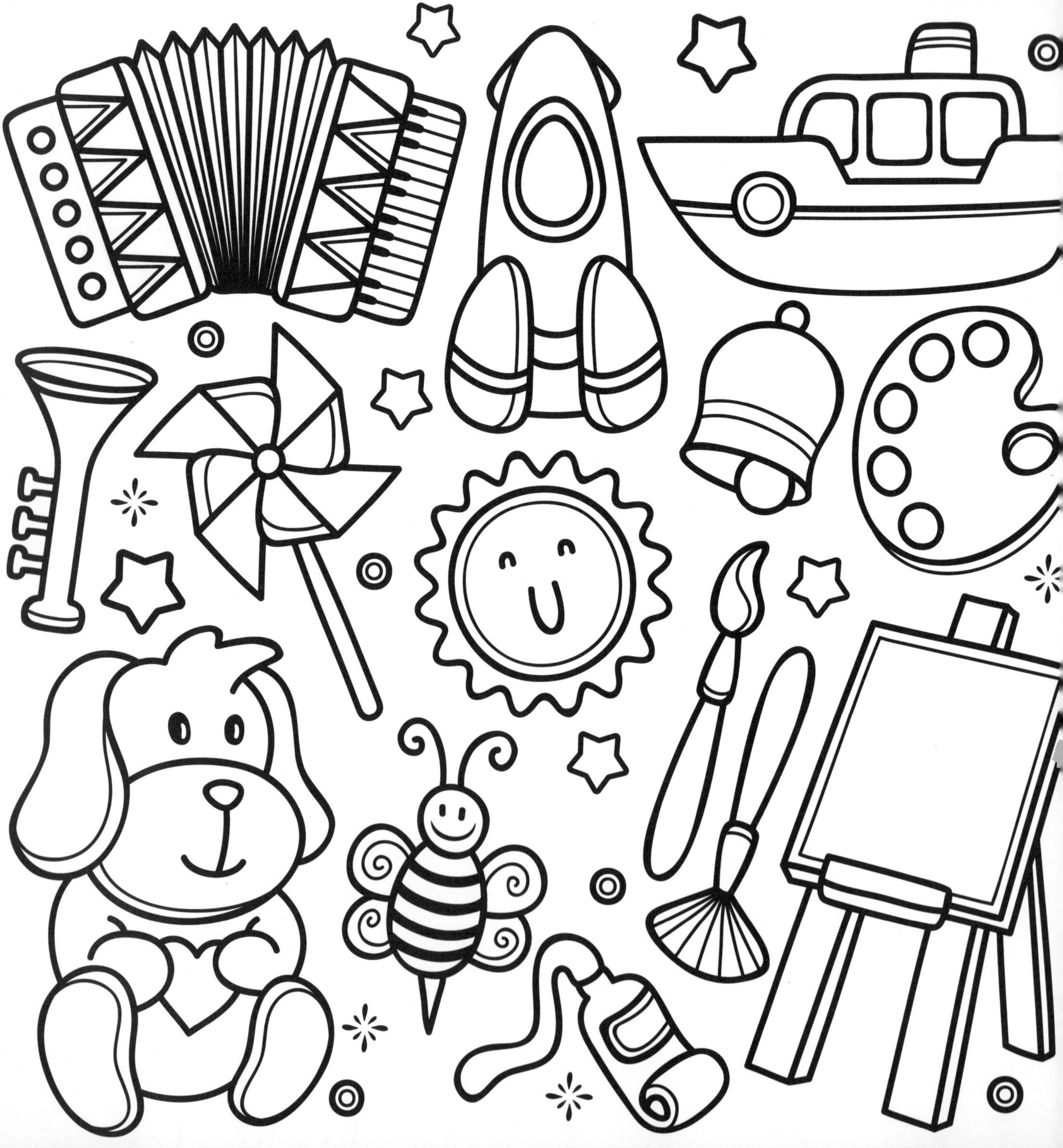

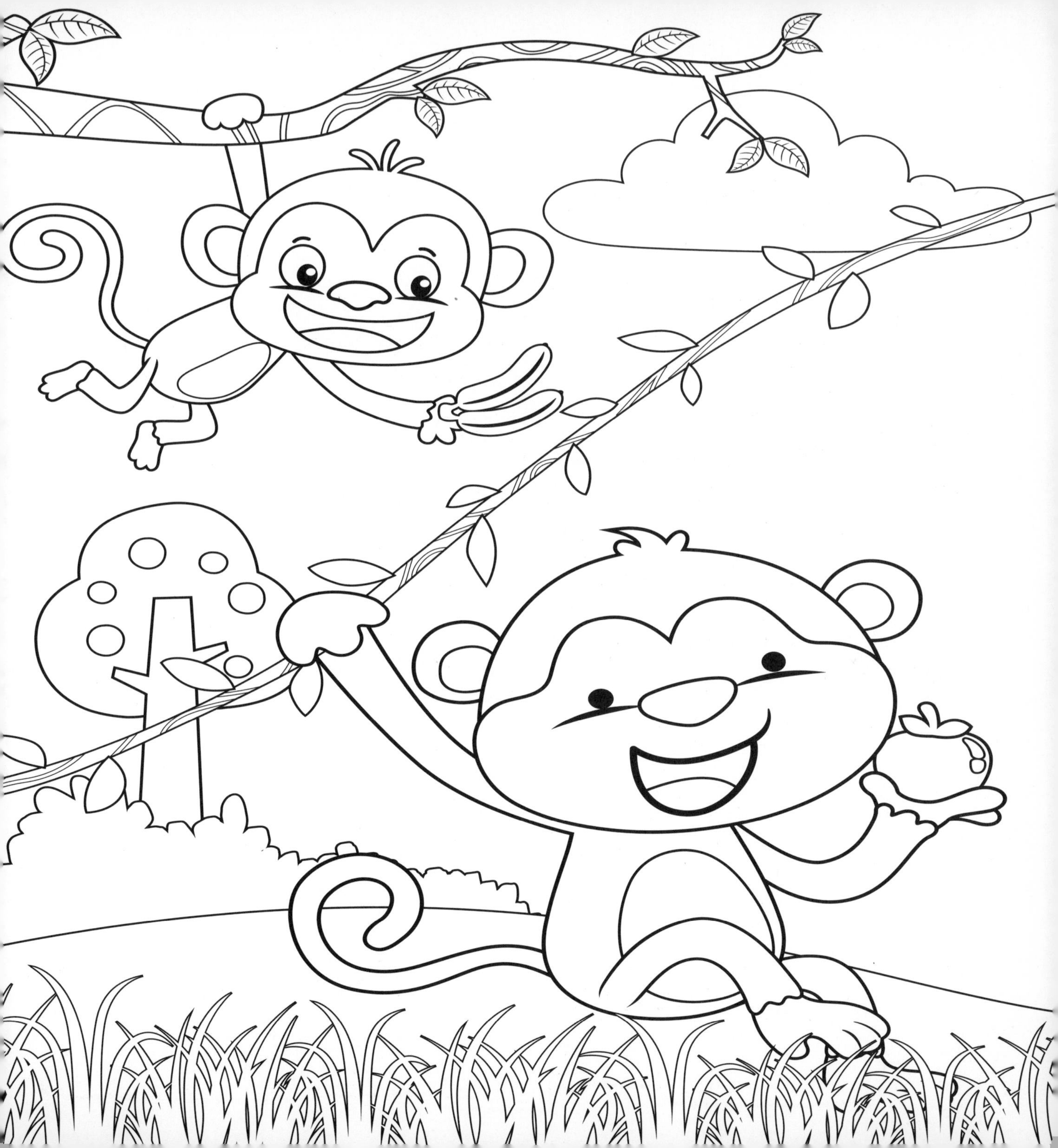

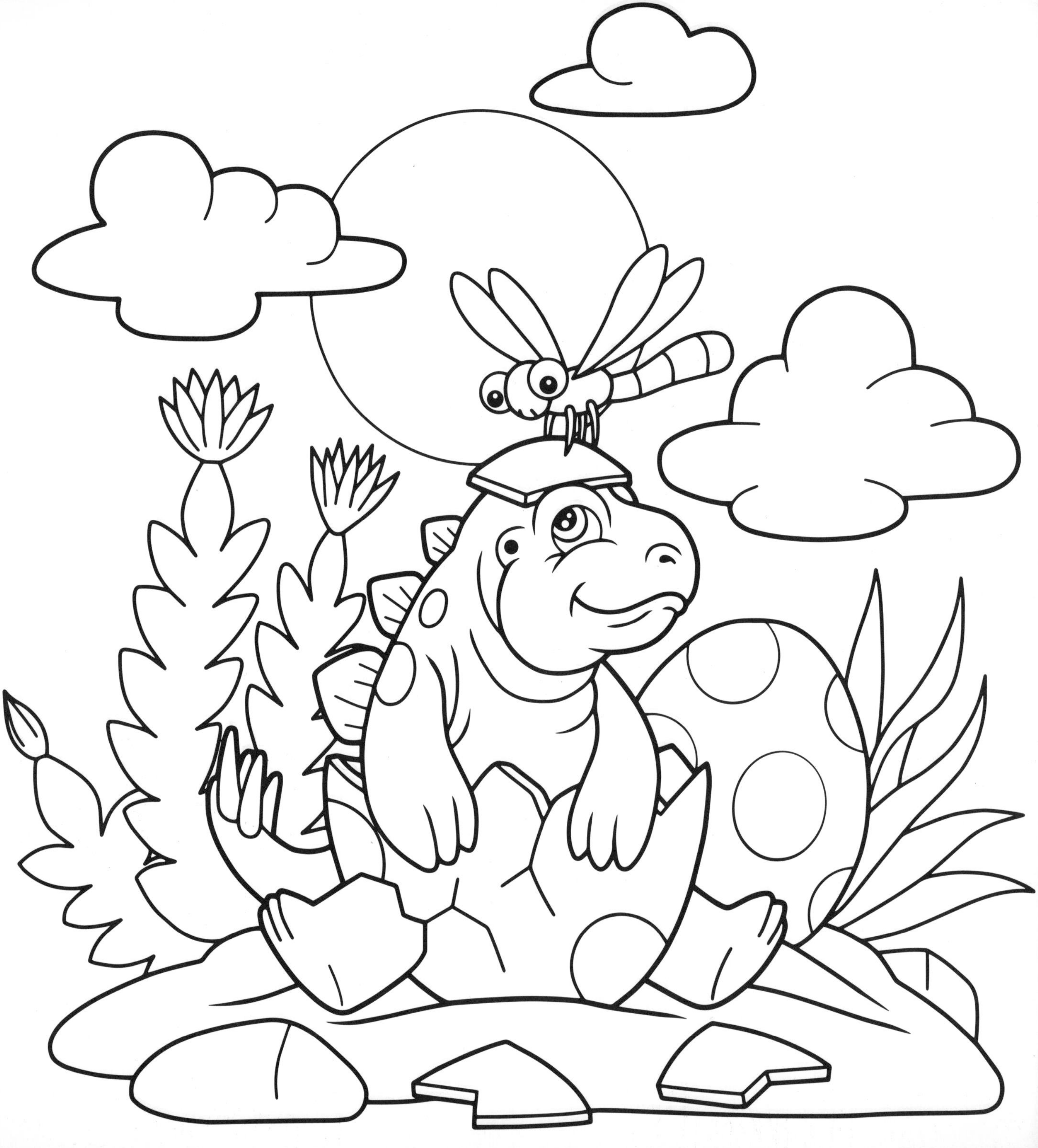

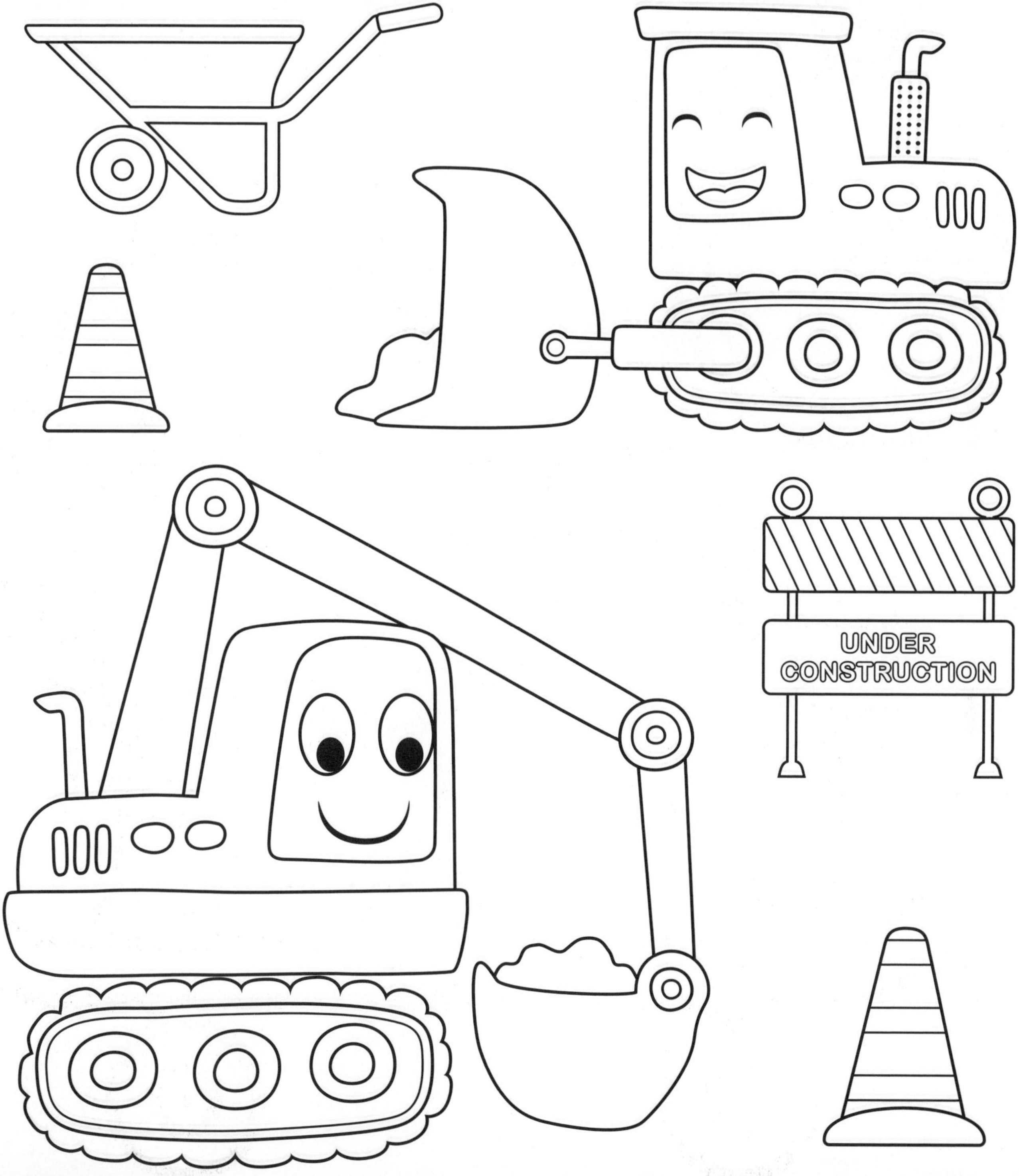
UNDER
CONSTRUCTION

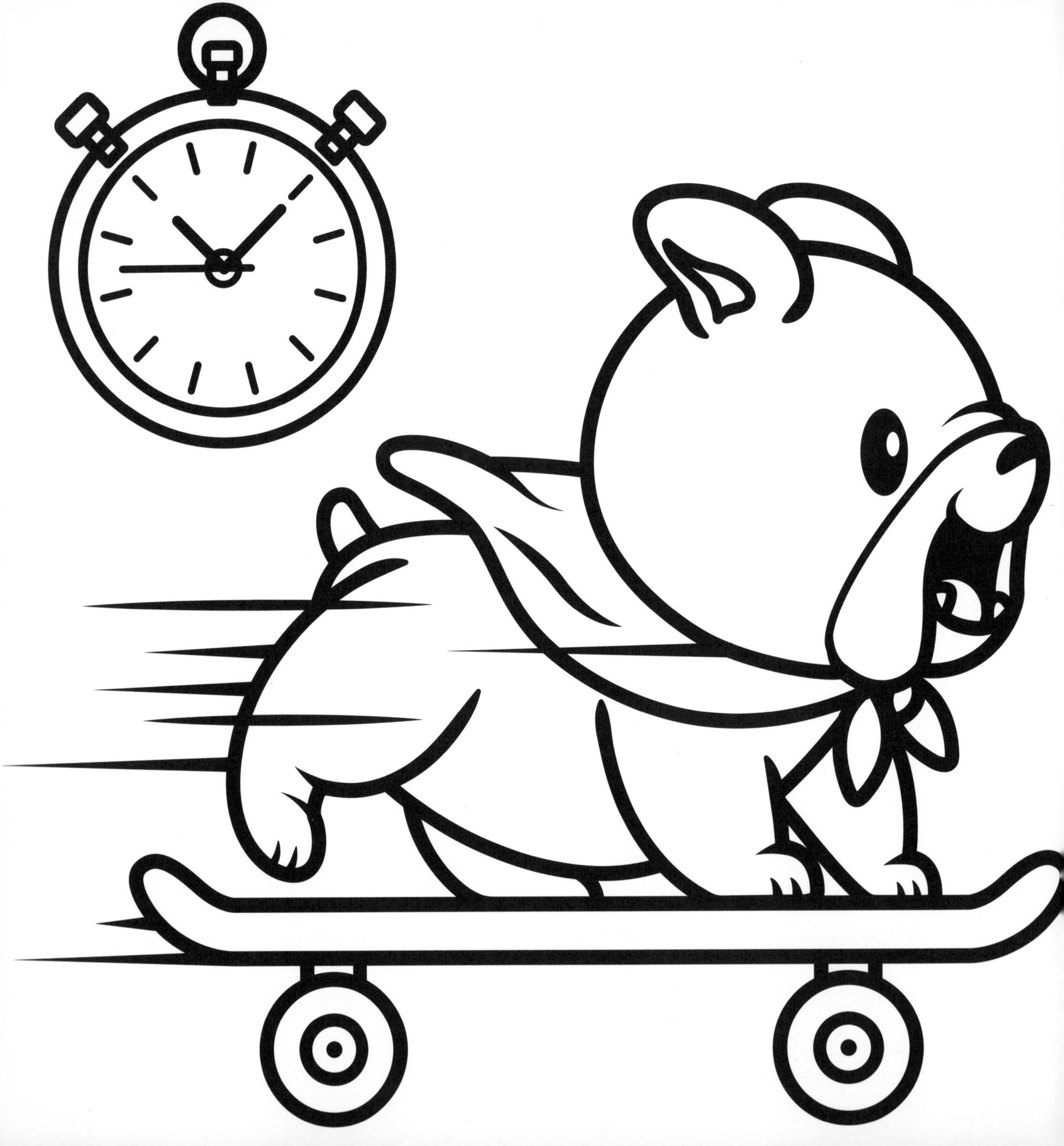

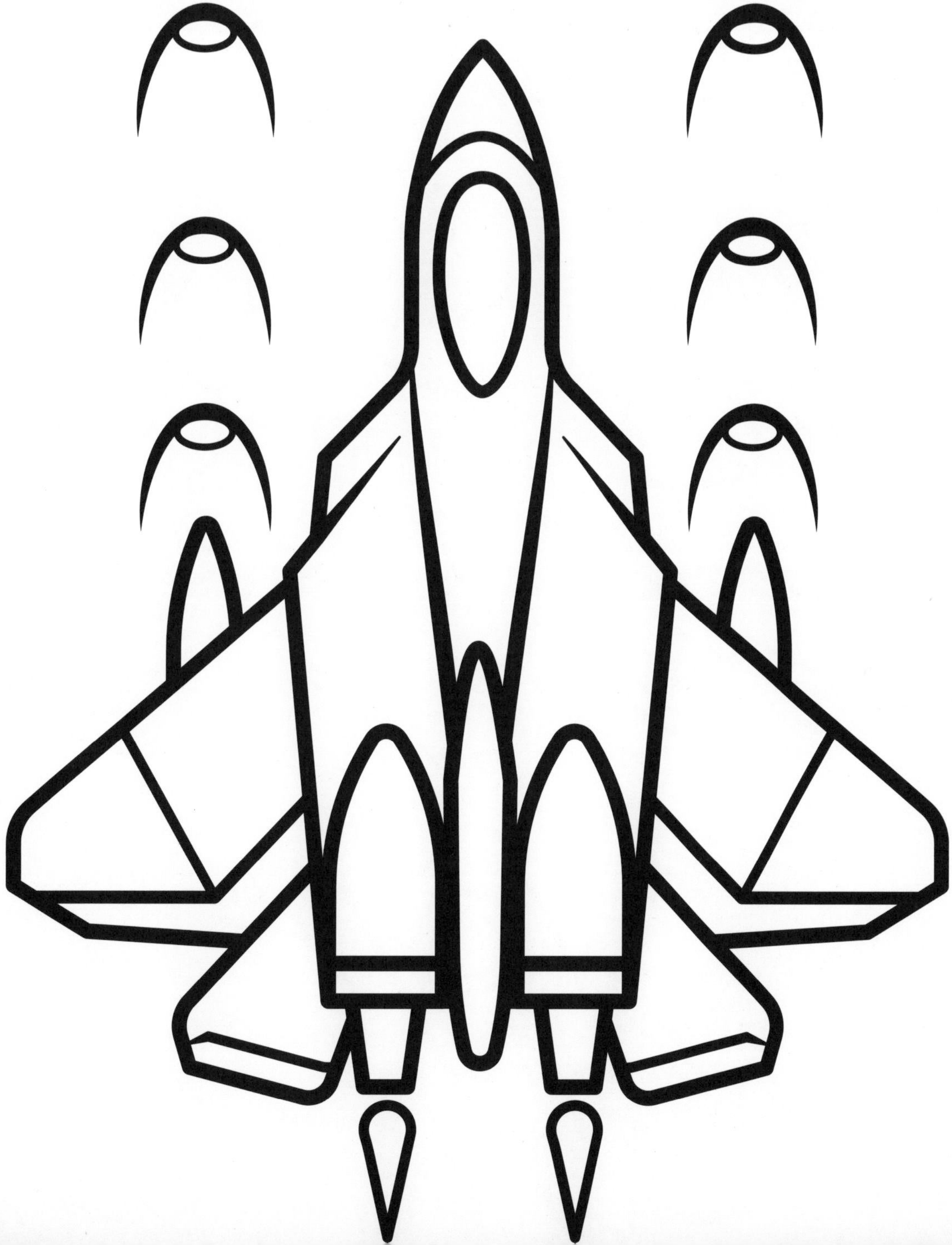

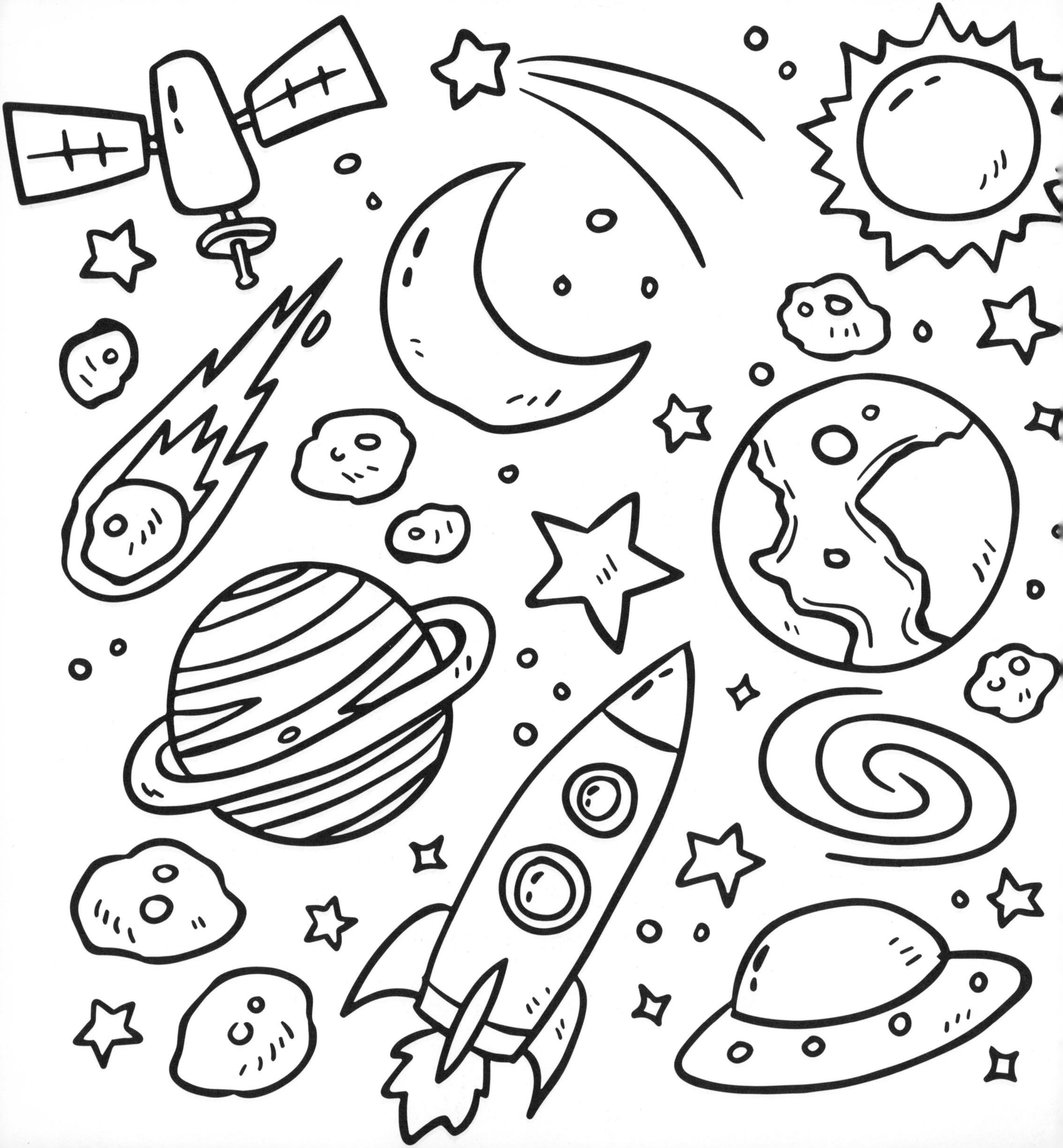

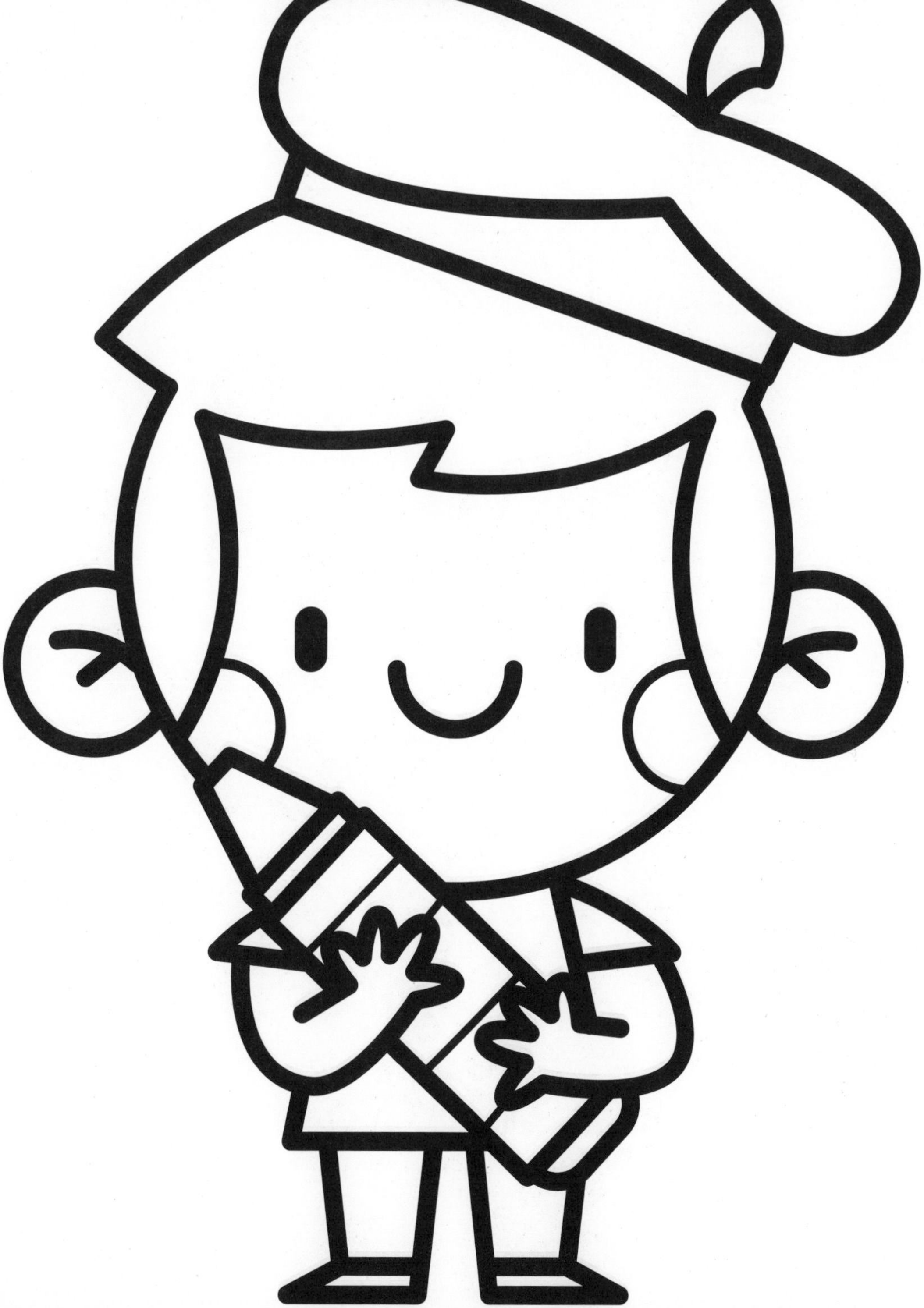

SPACE

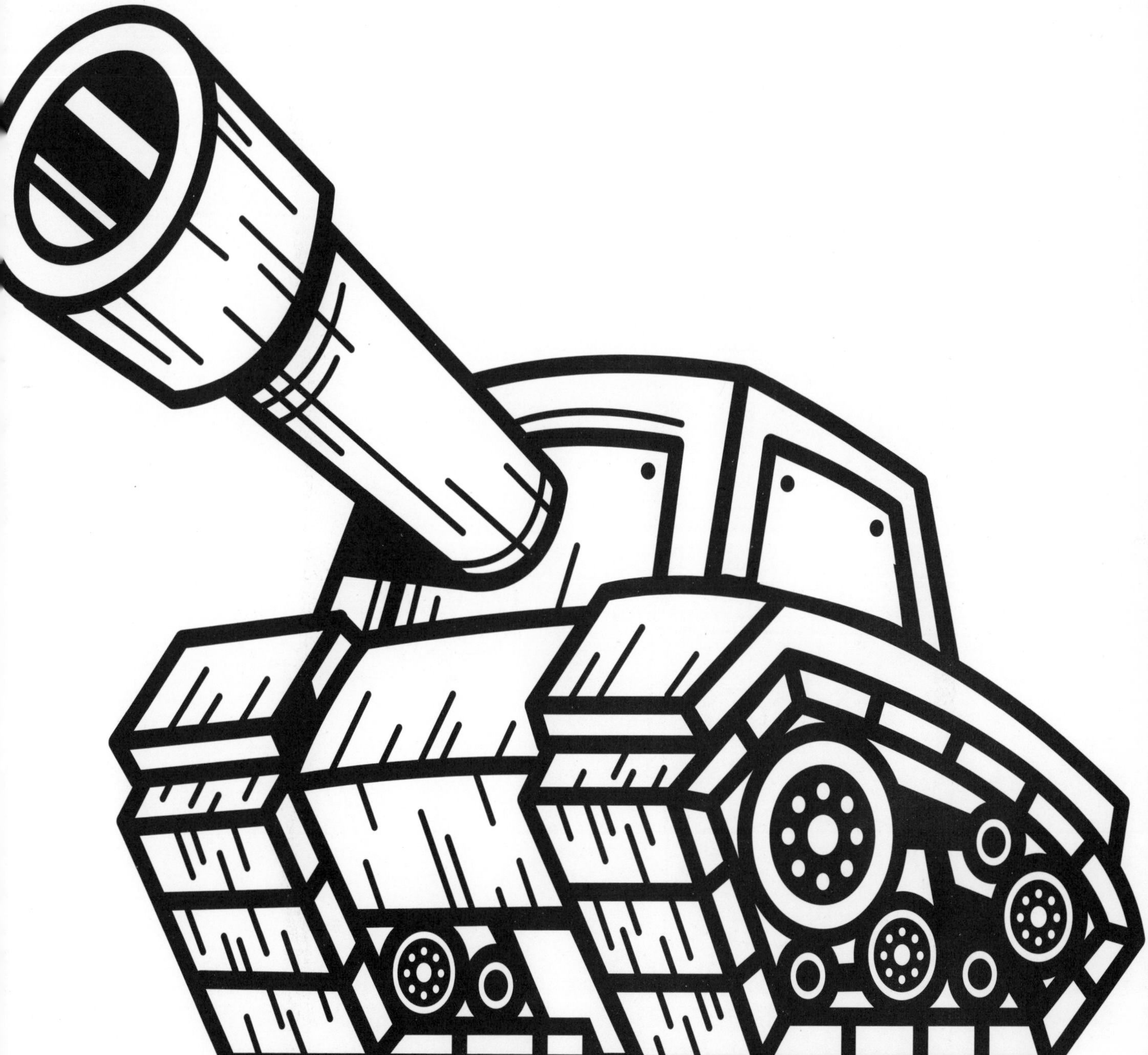

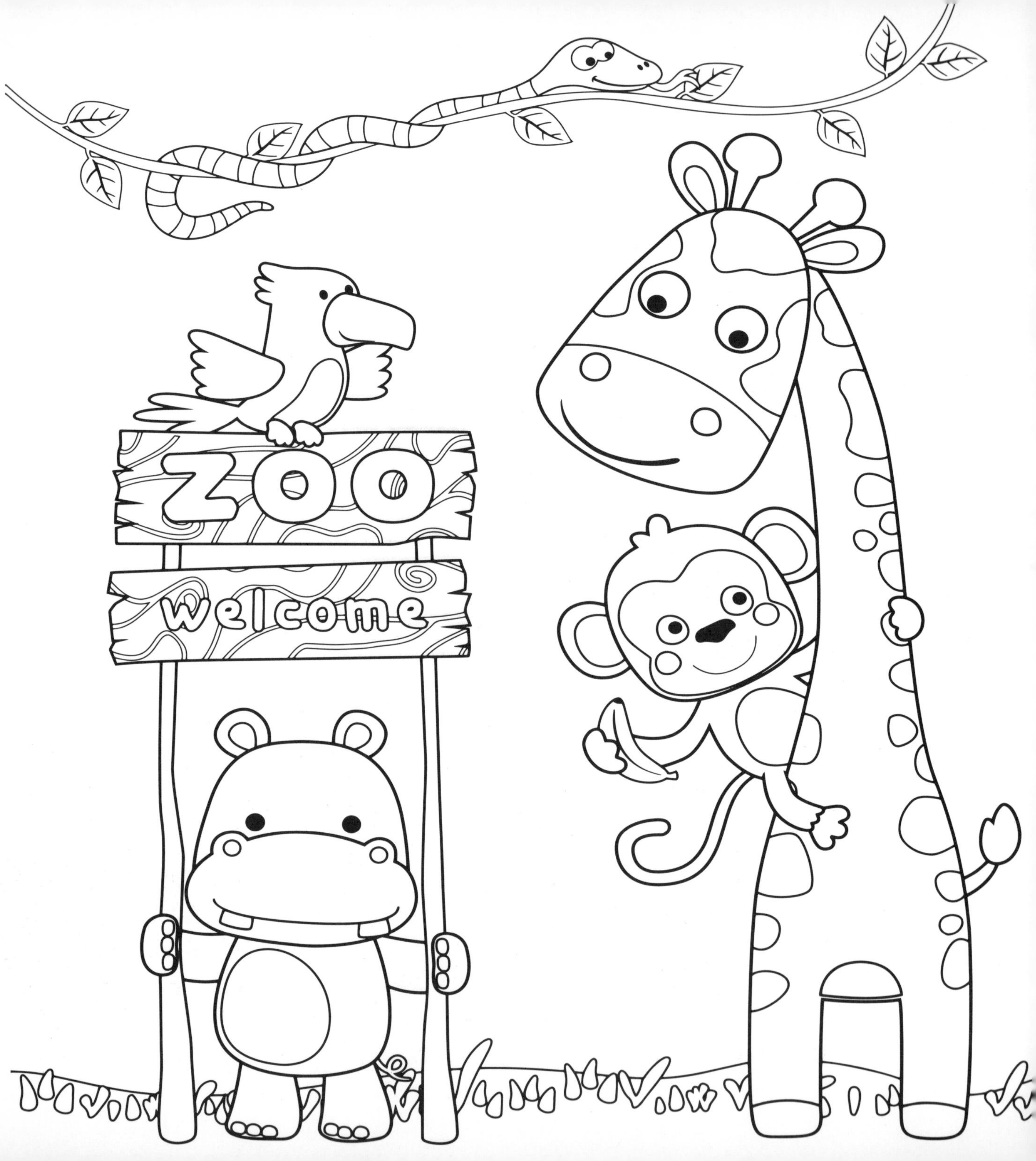
ZOO
welcome

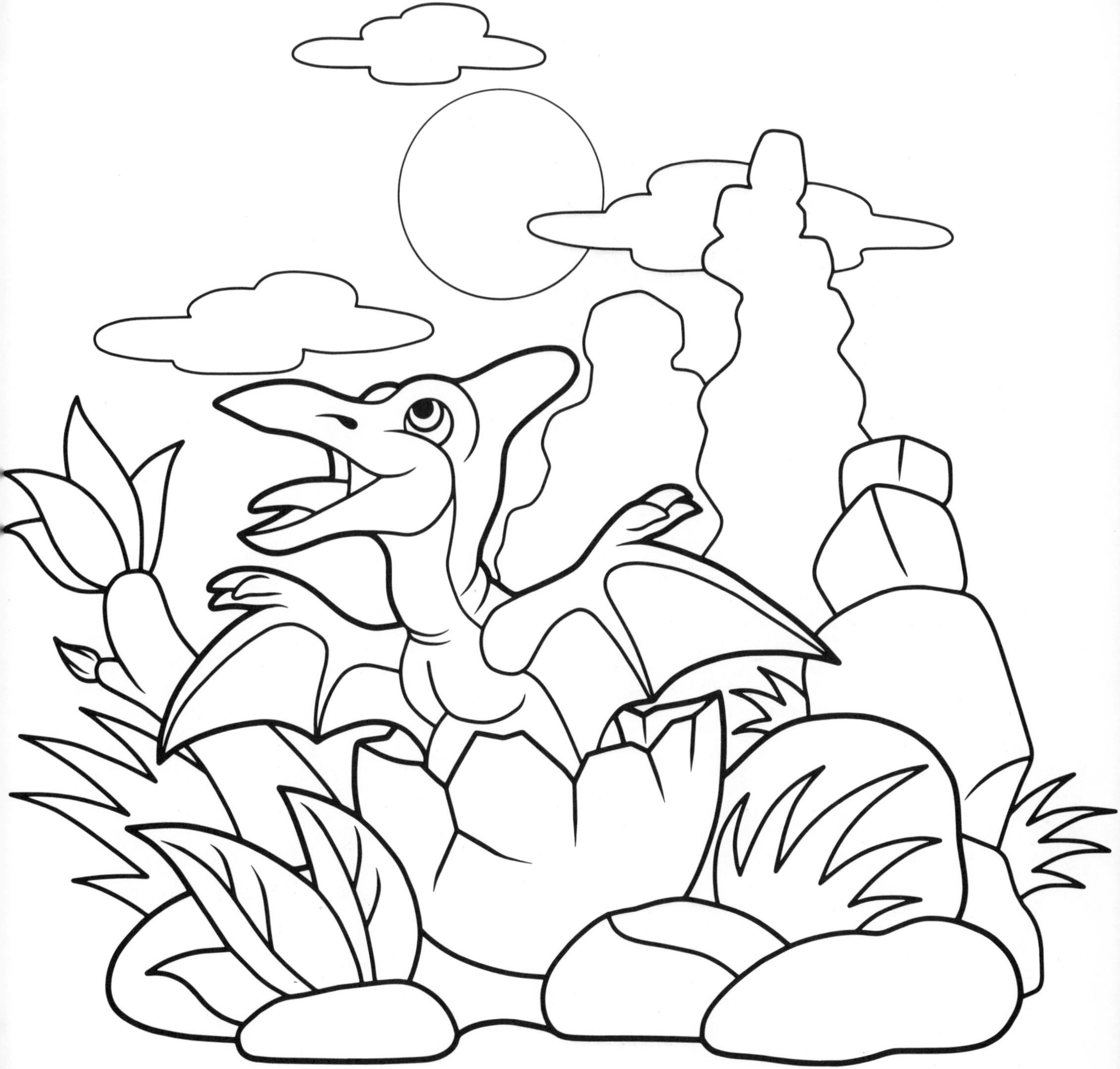

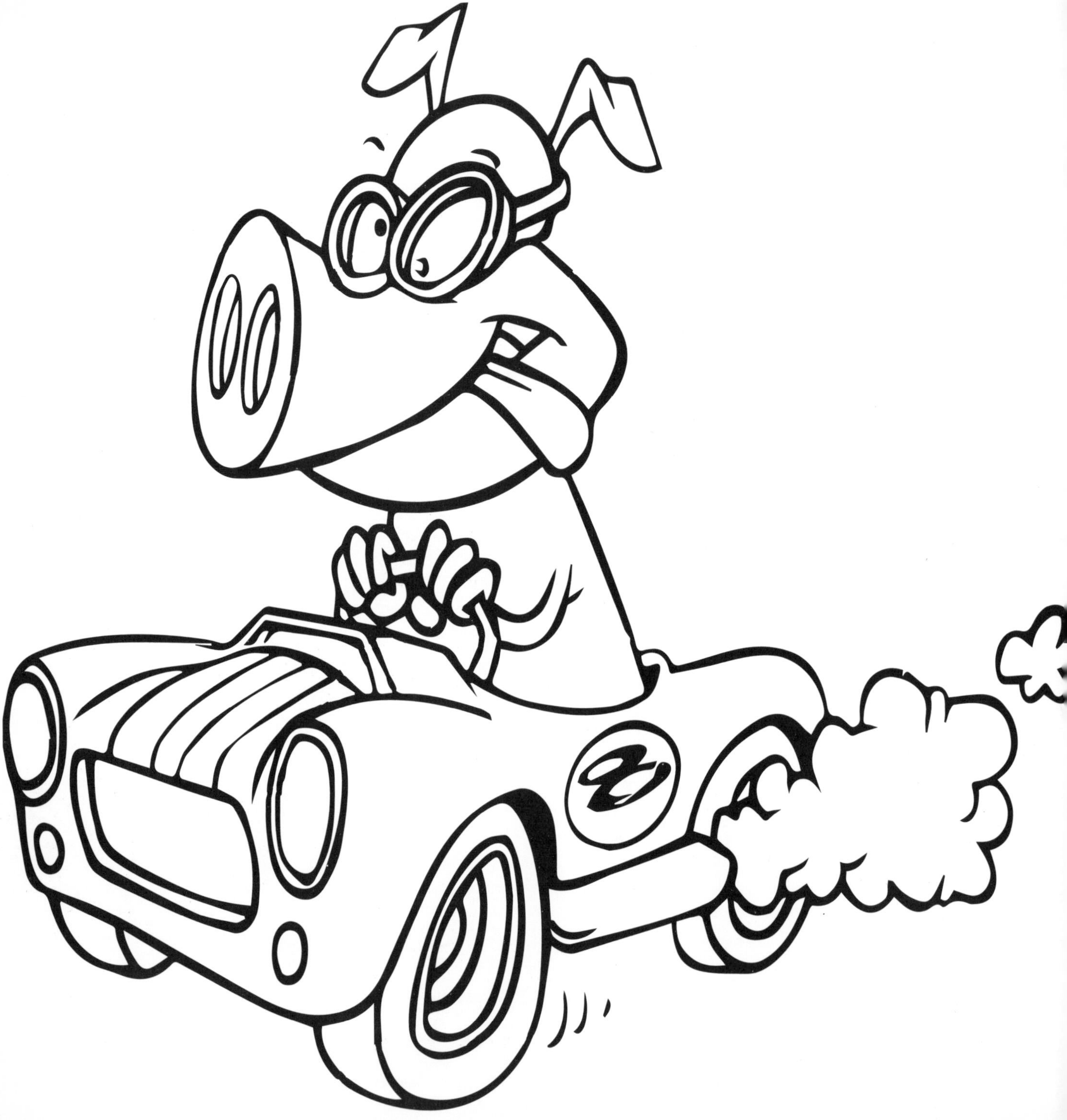

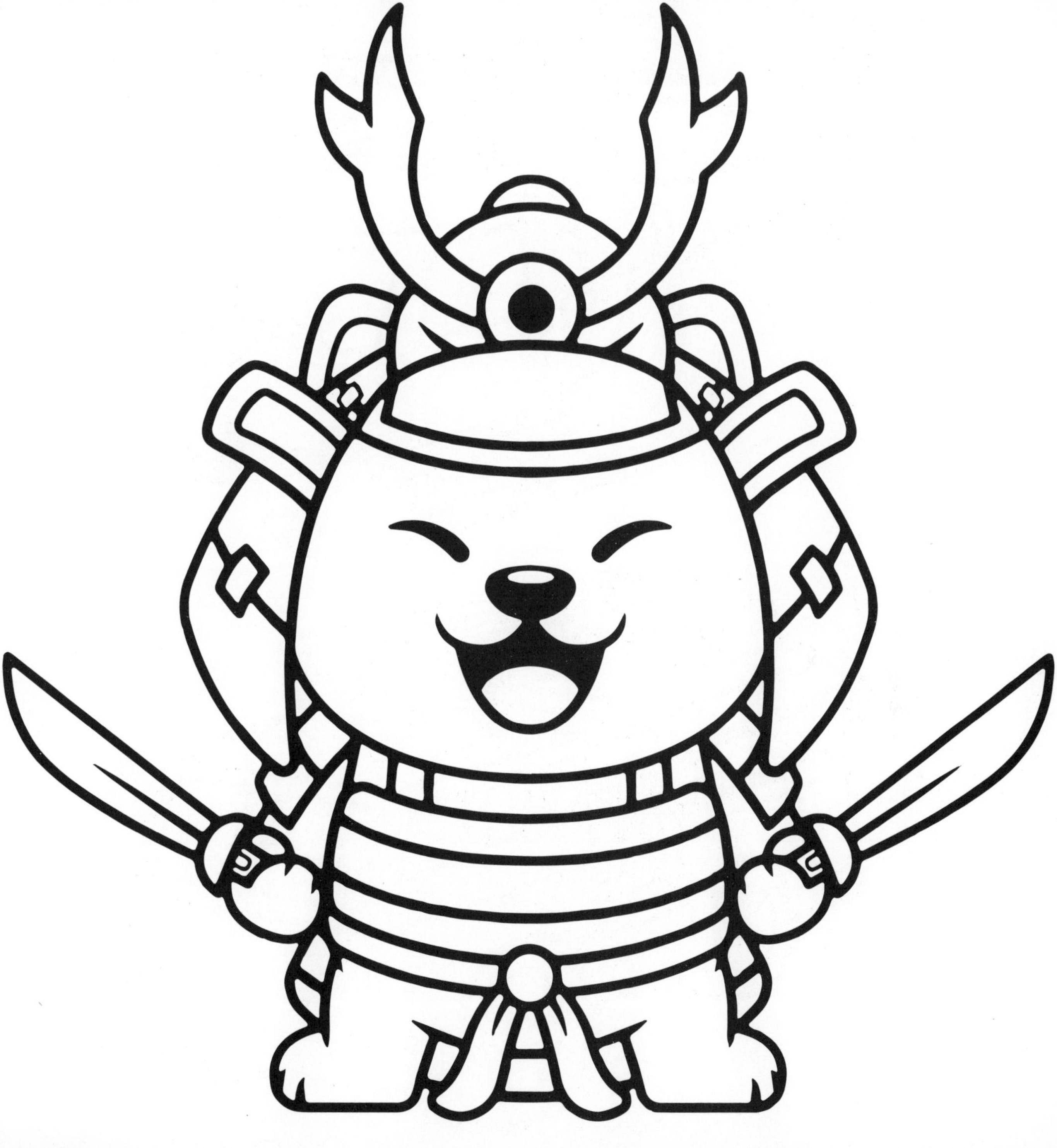

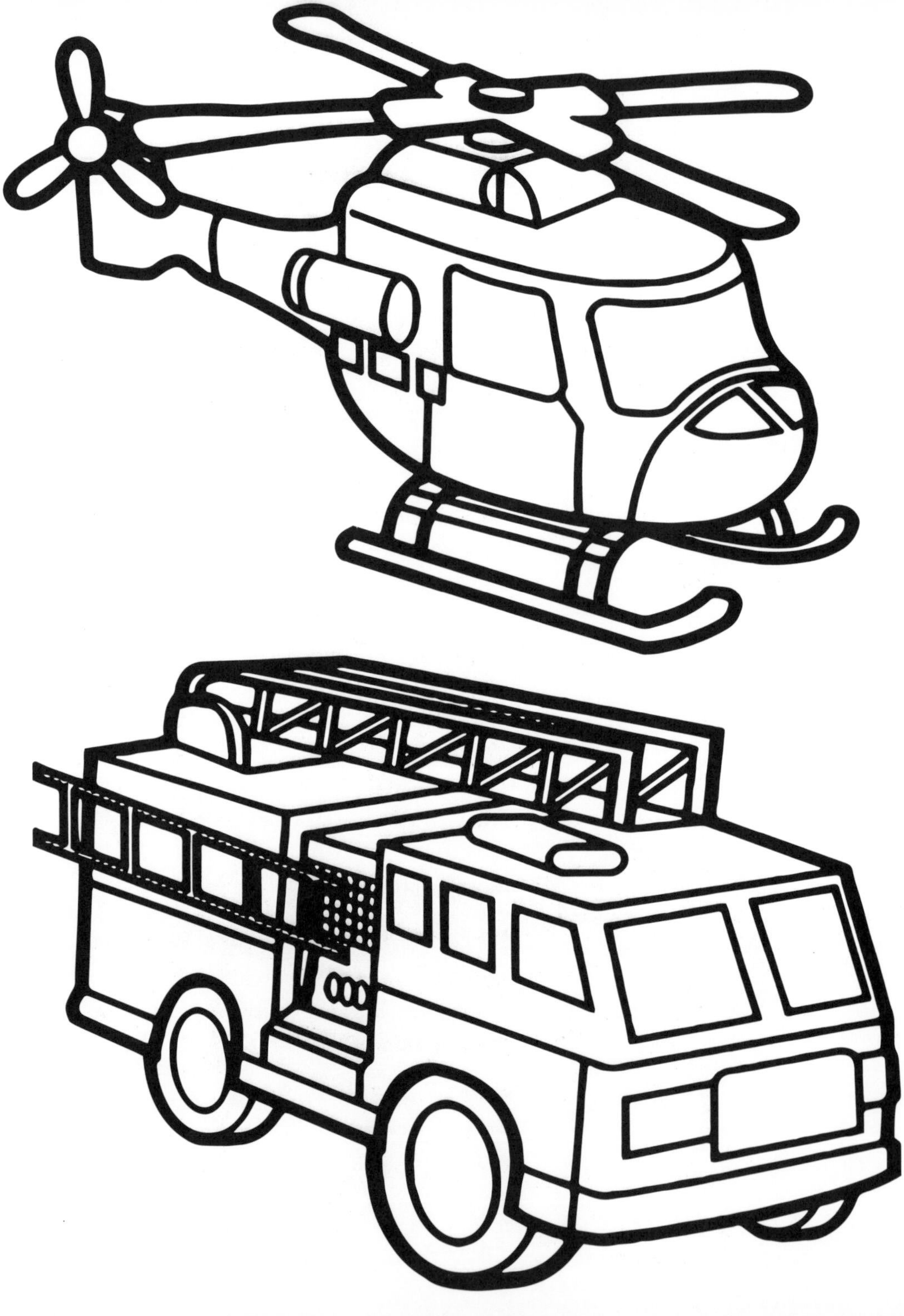

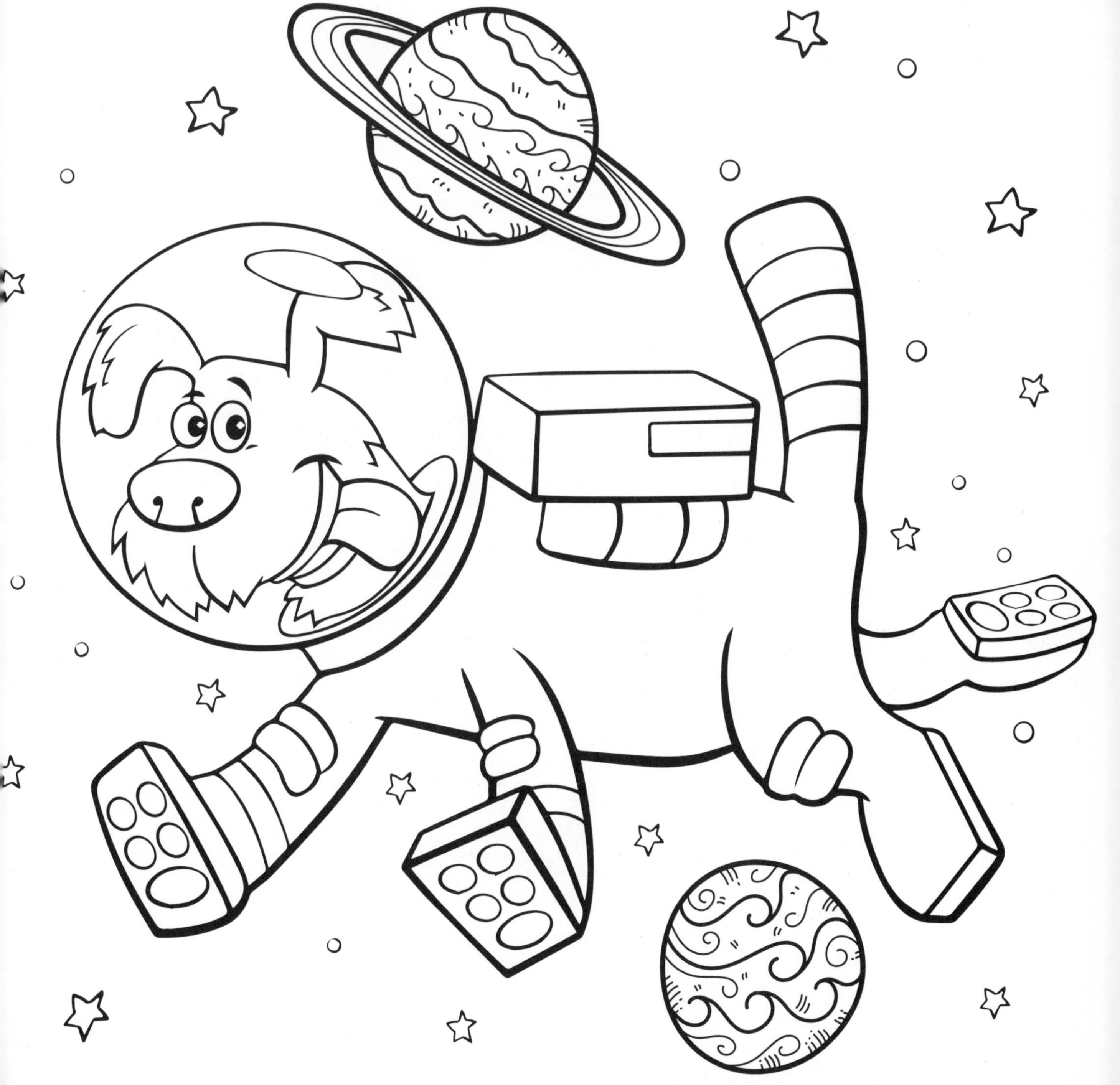

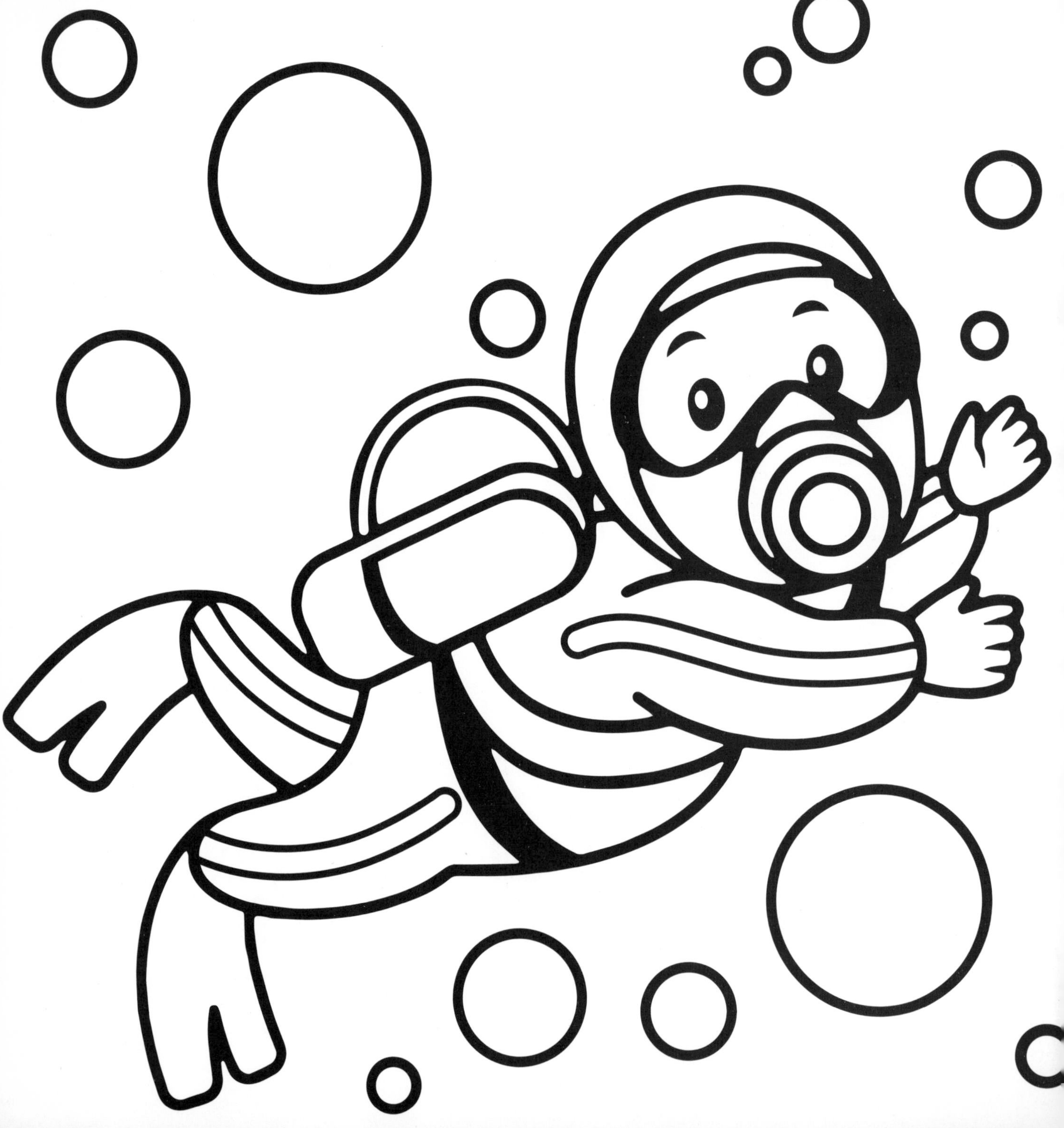

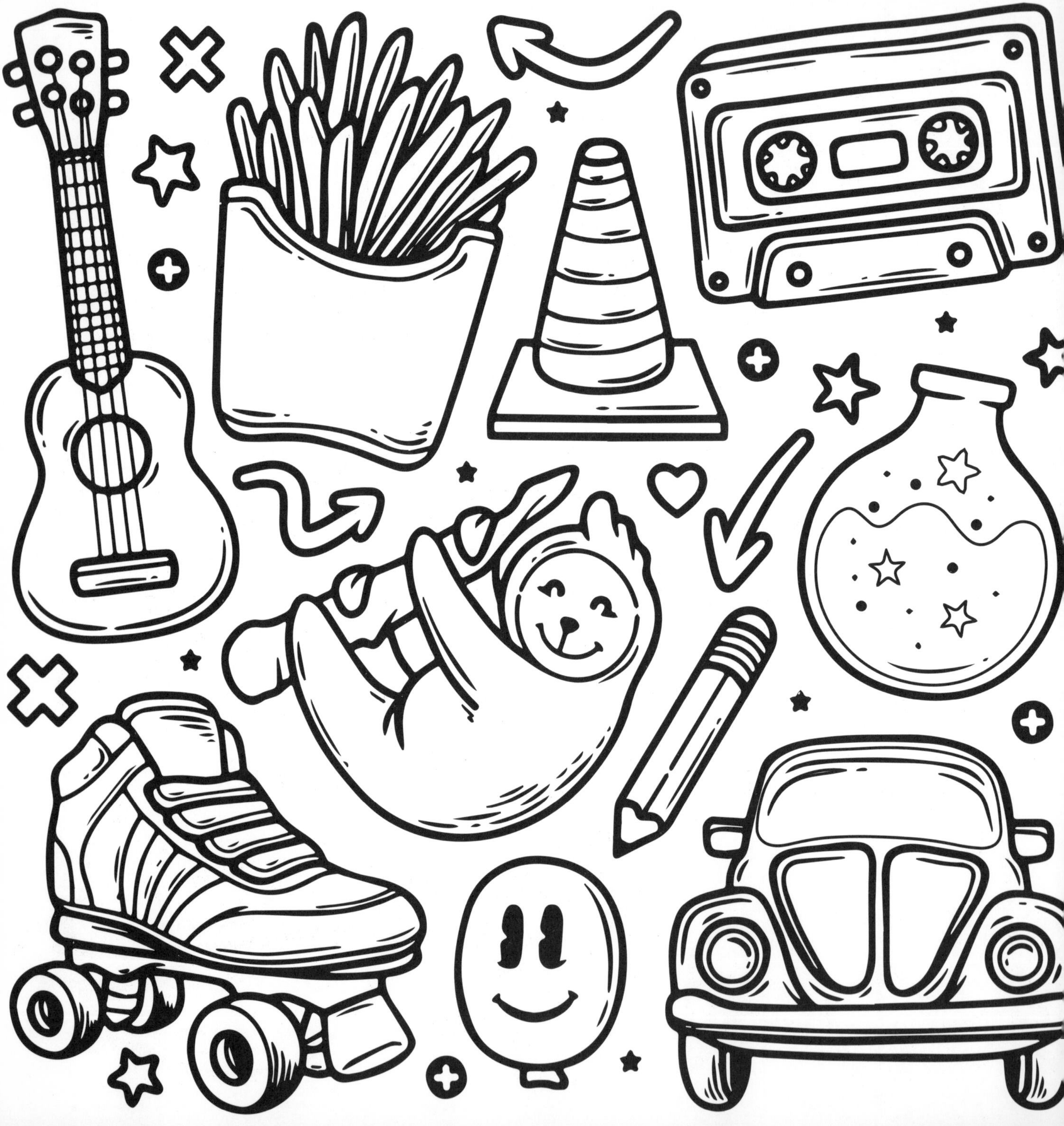

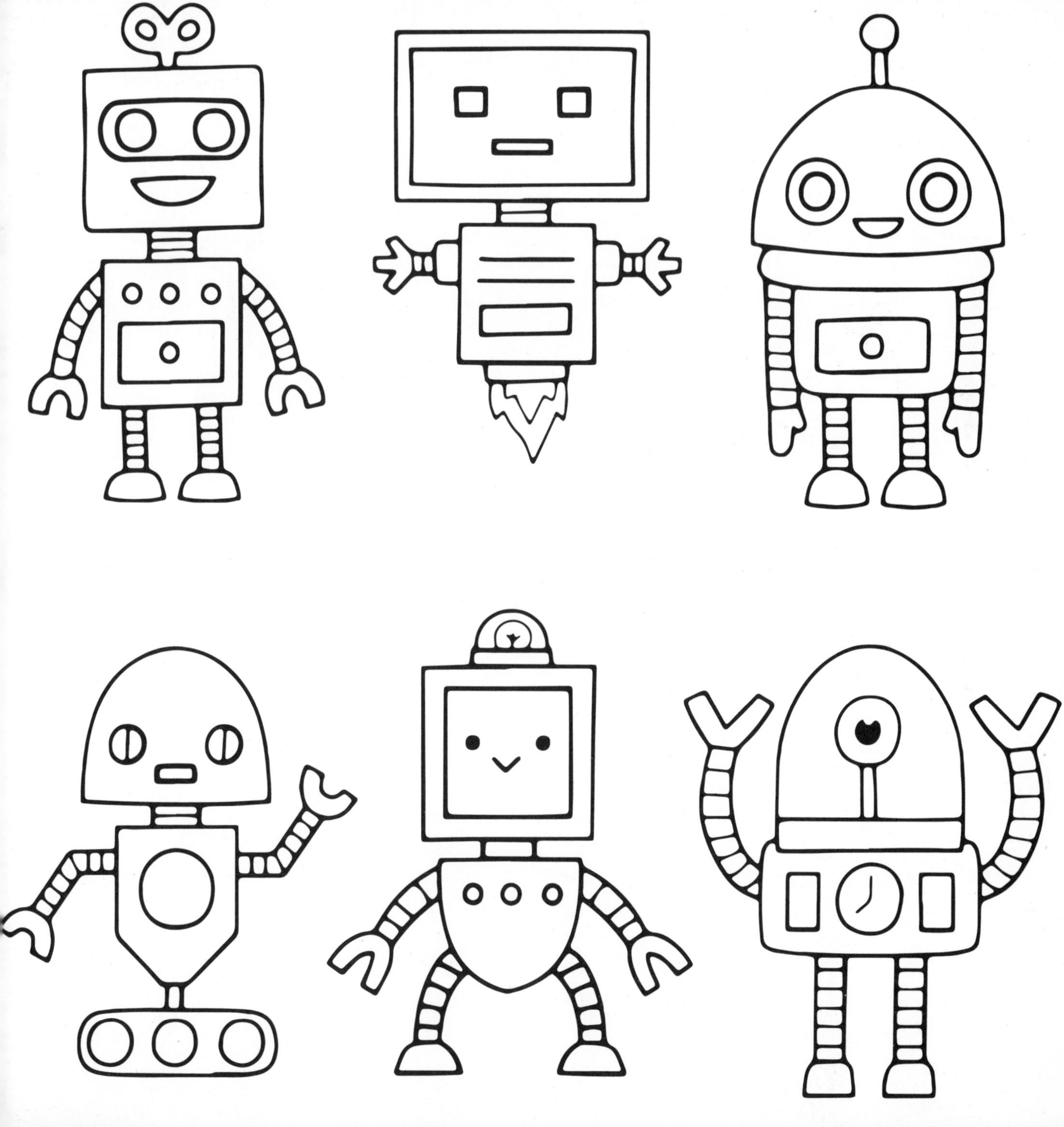

Space
UFO
UFO
UFO

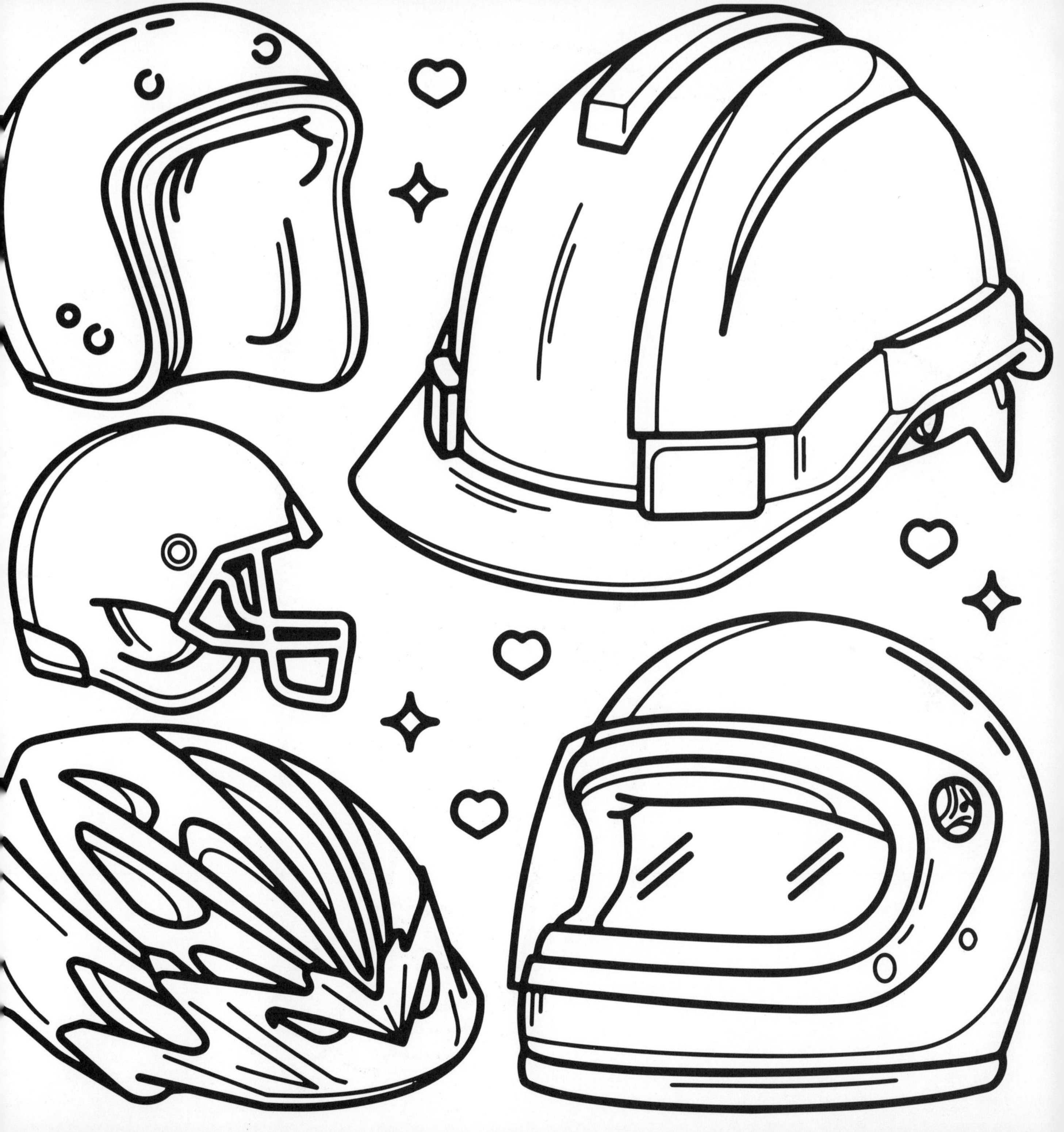

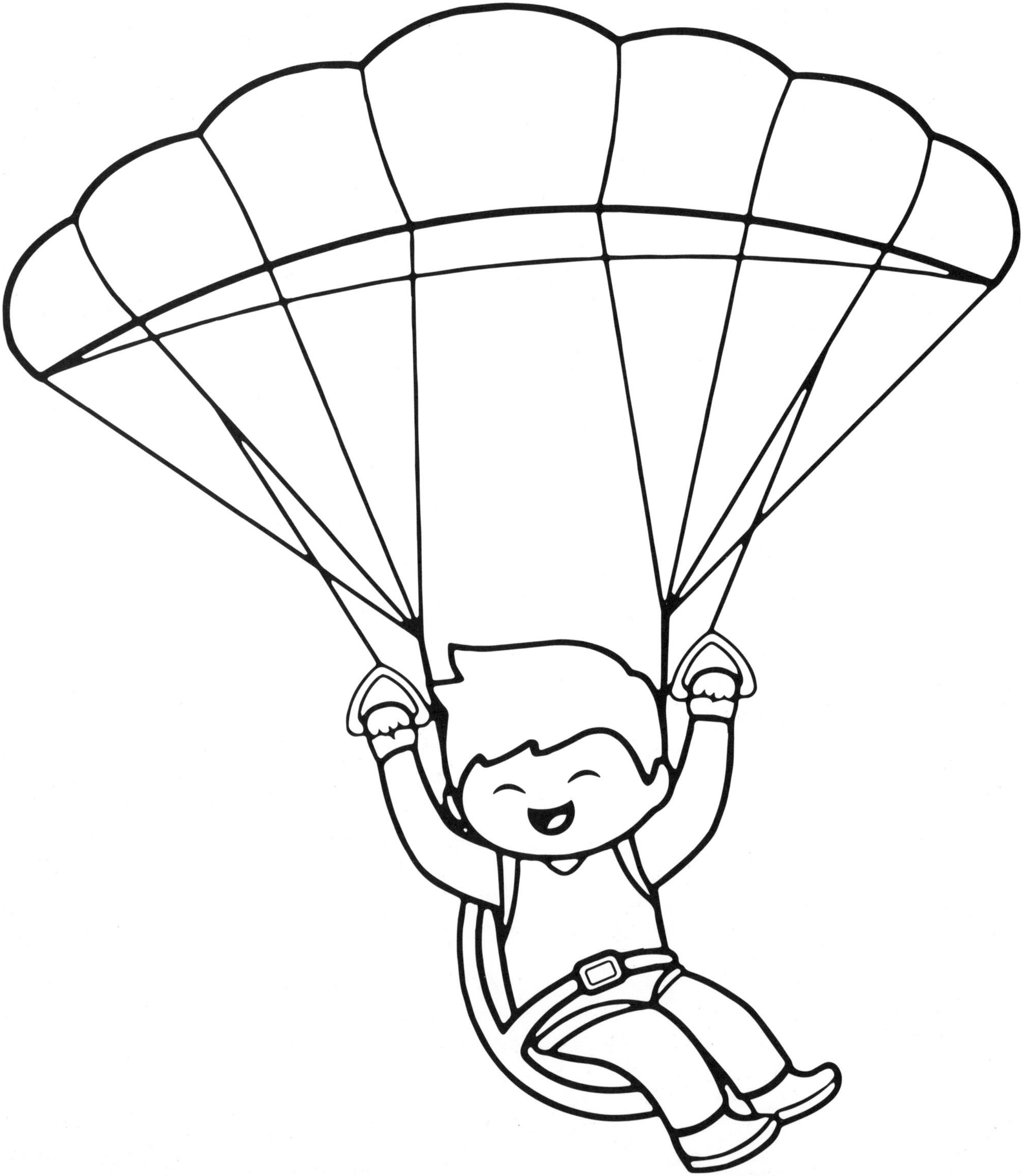

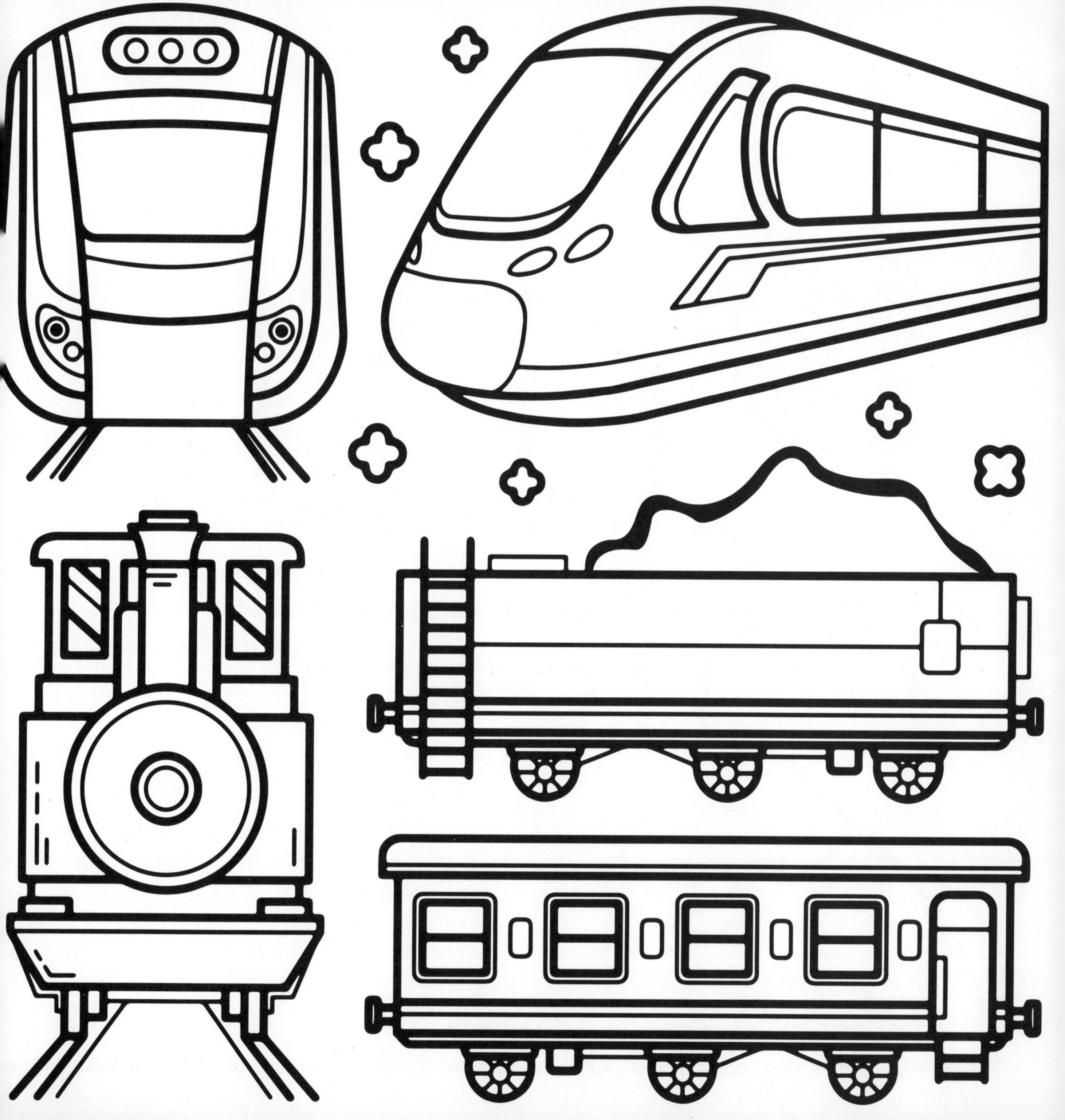

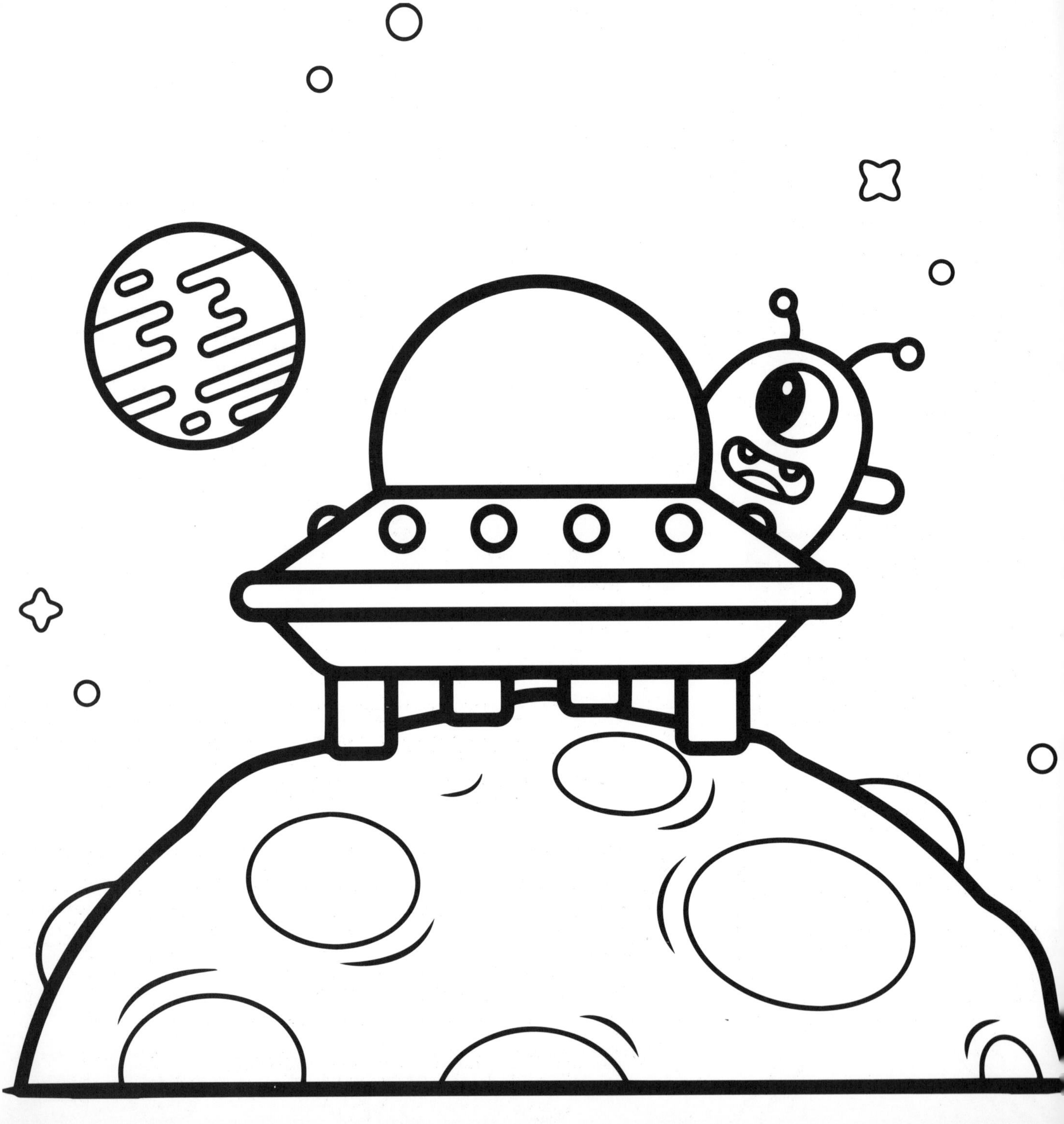

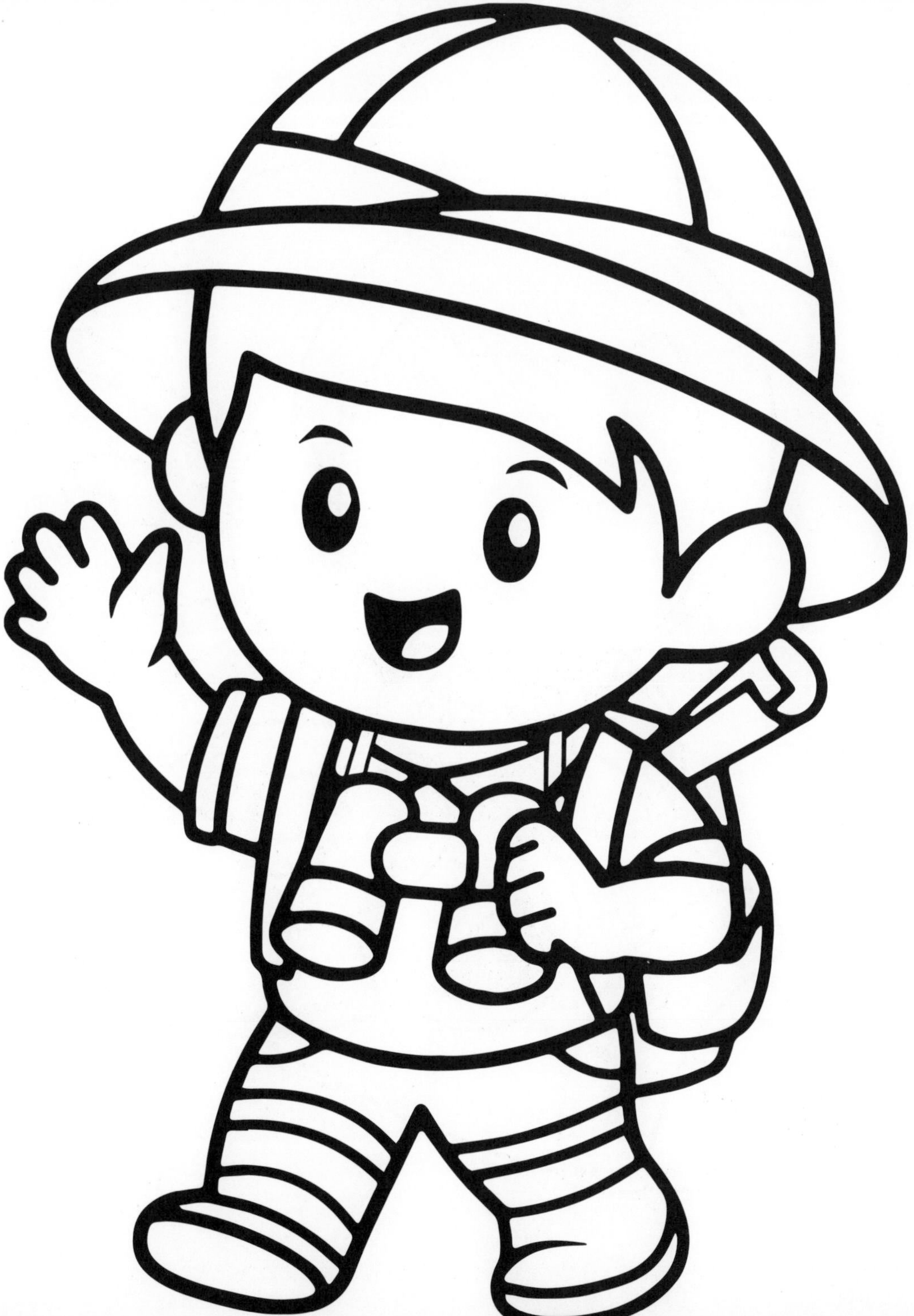

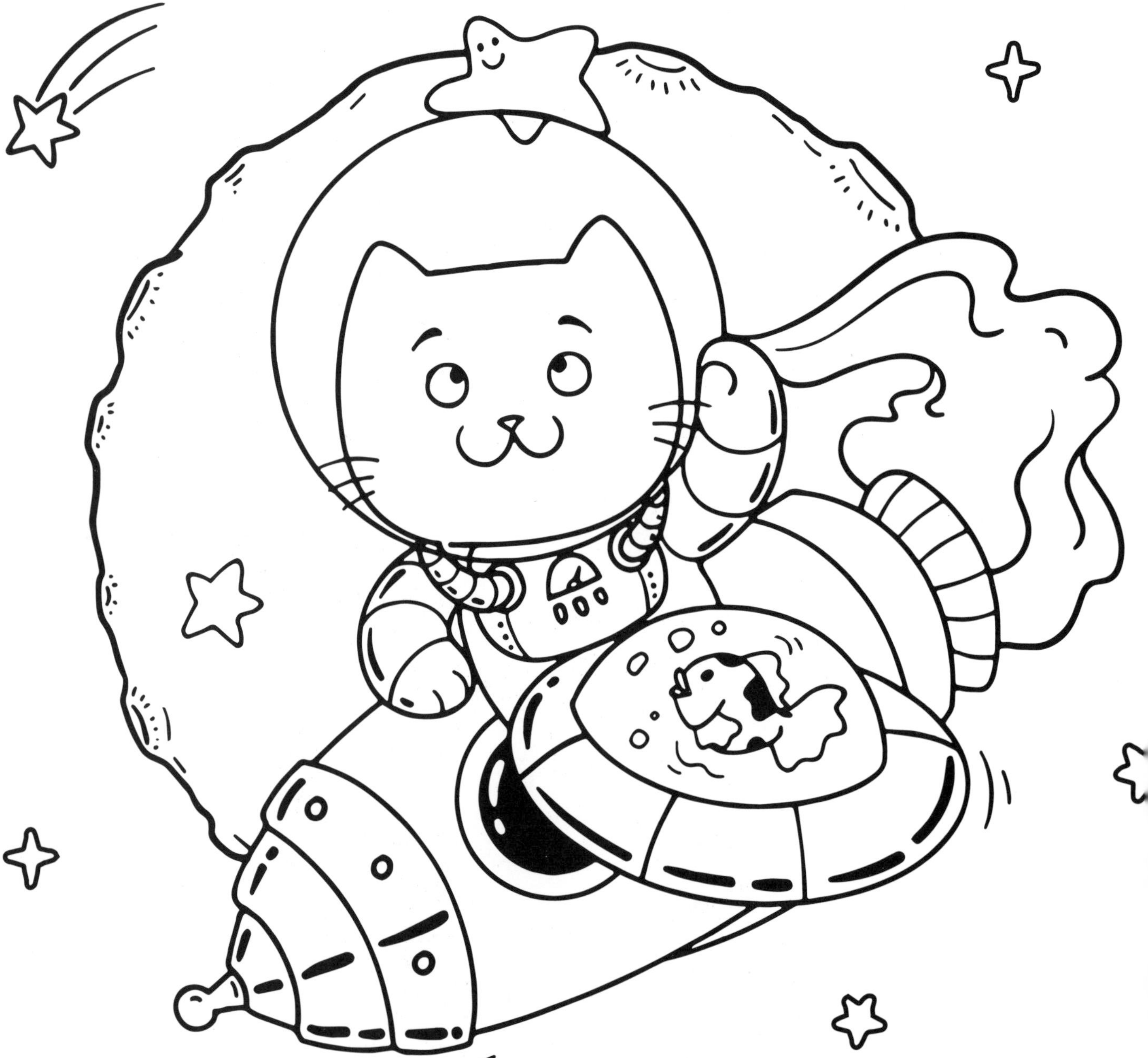

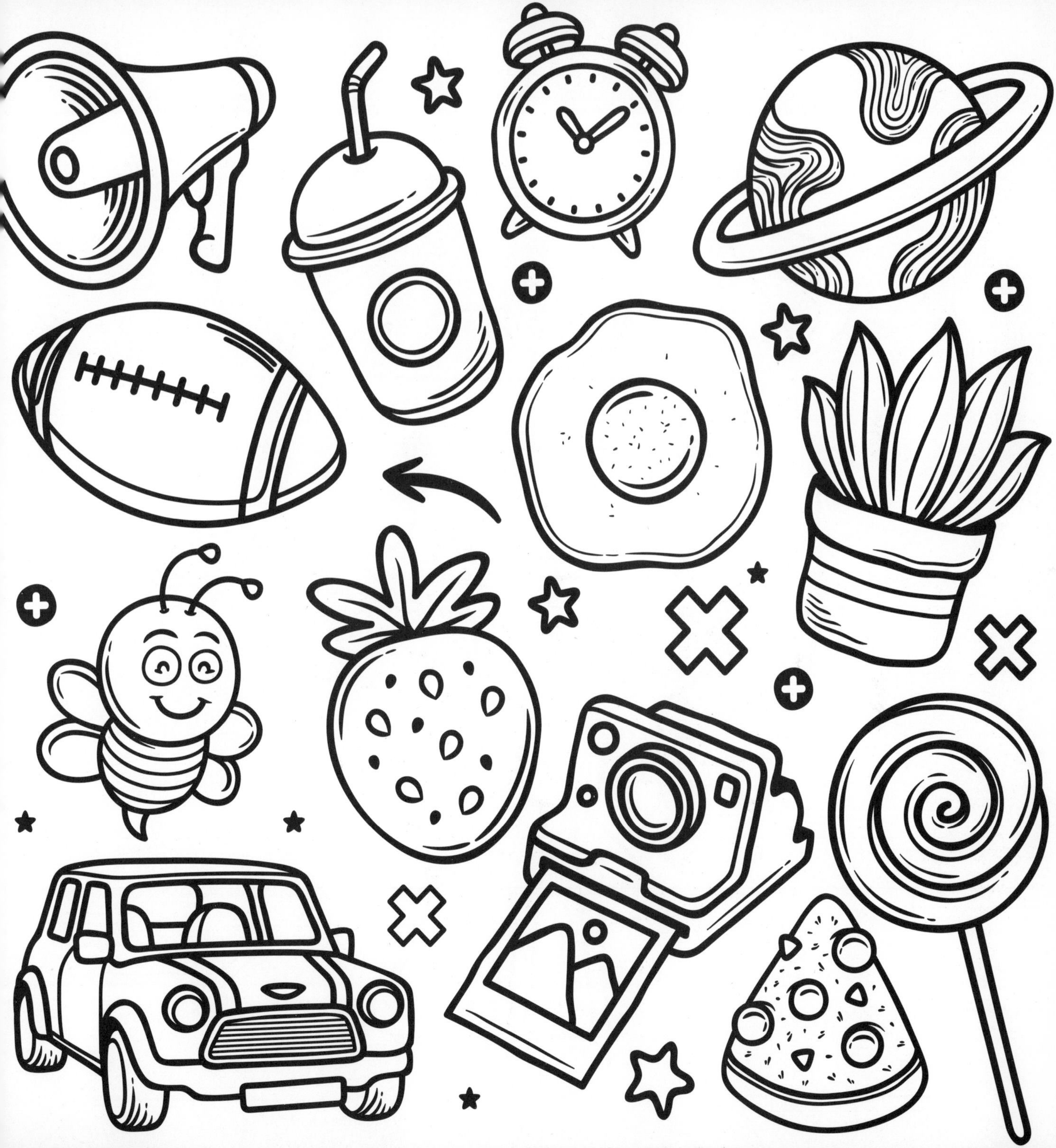

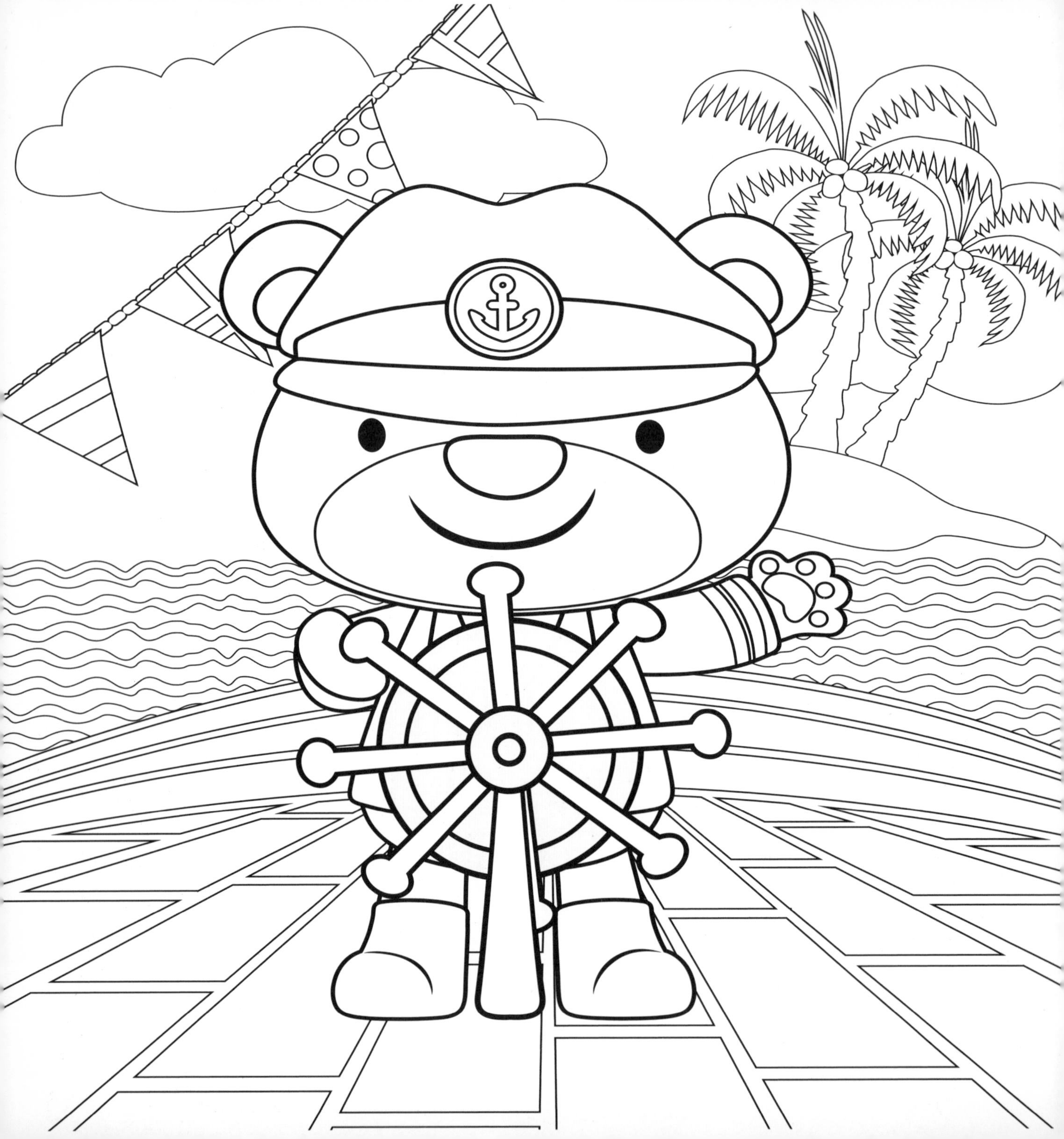

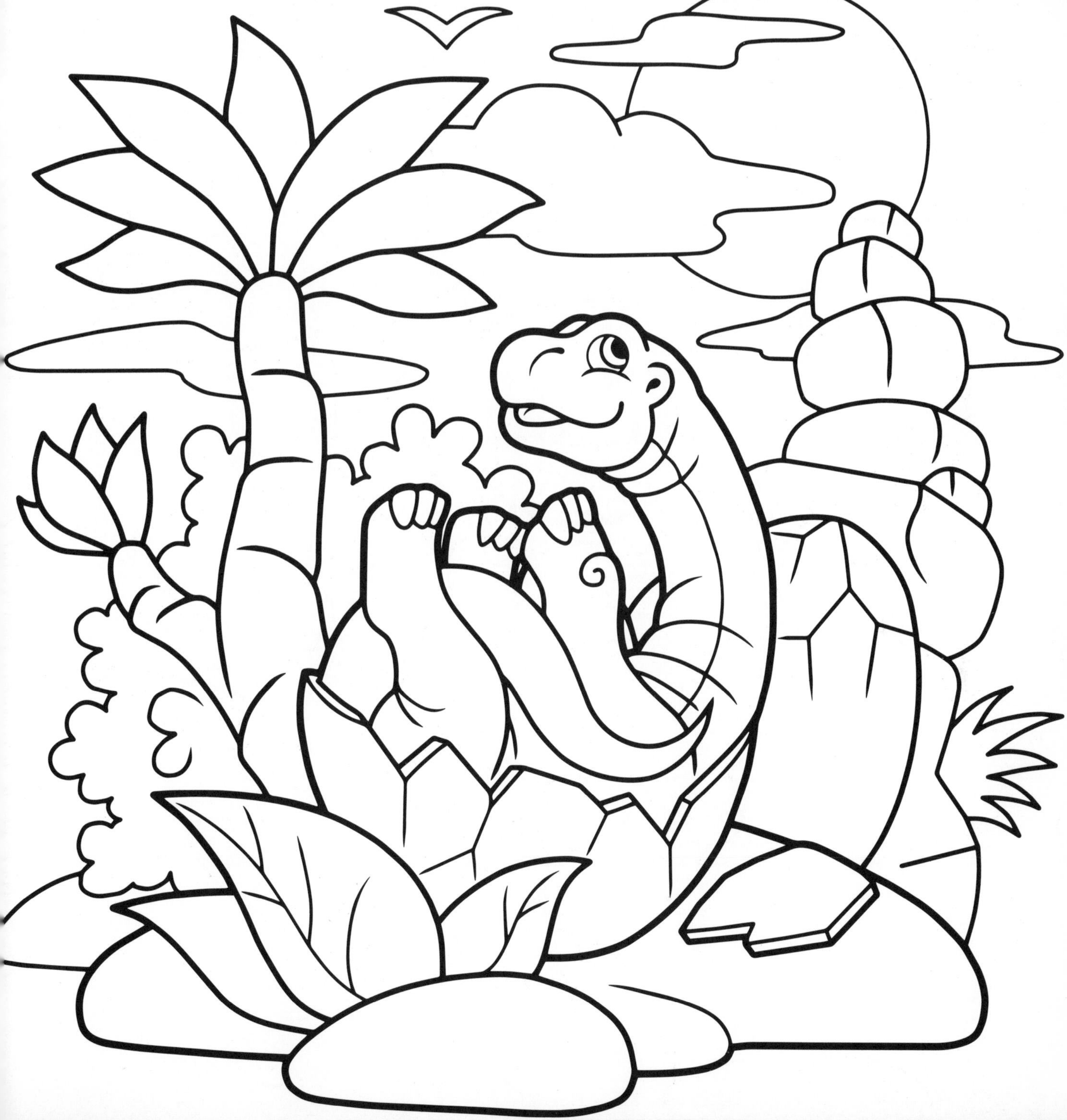

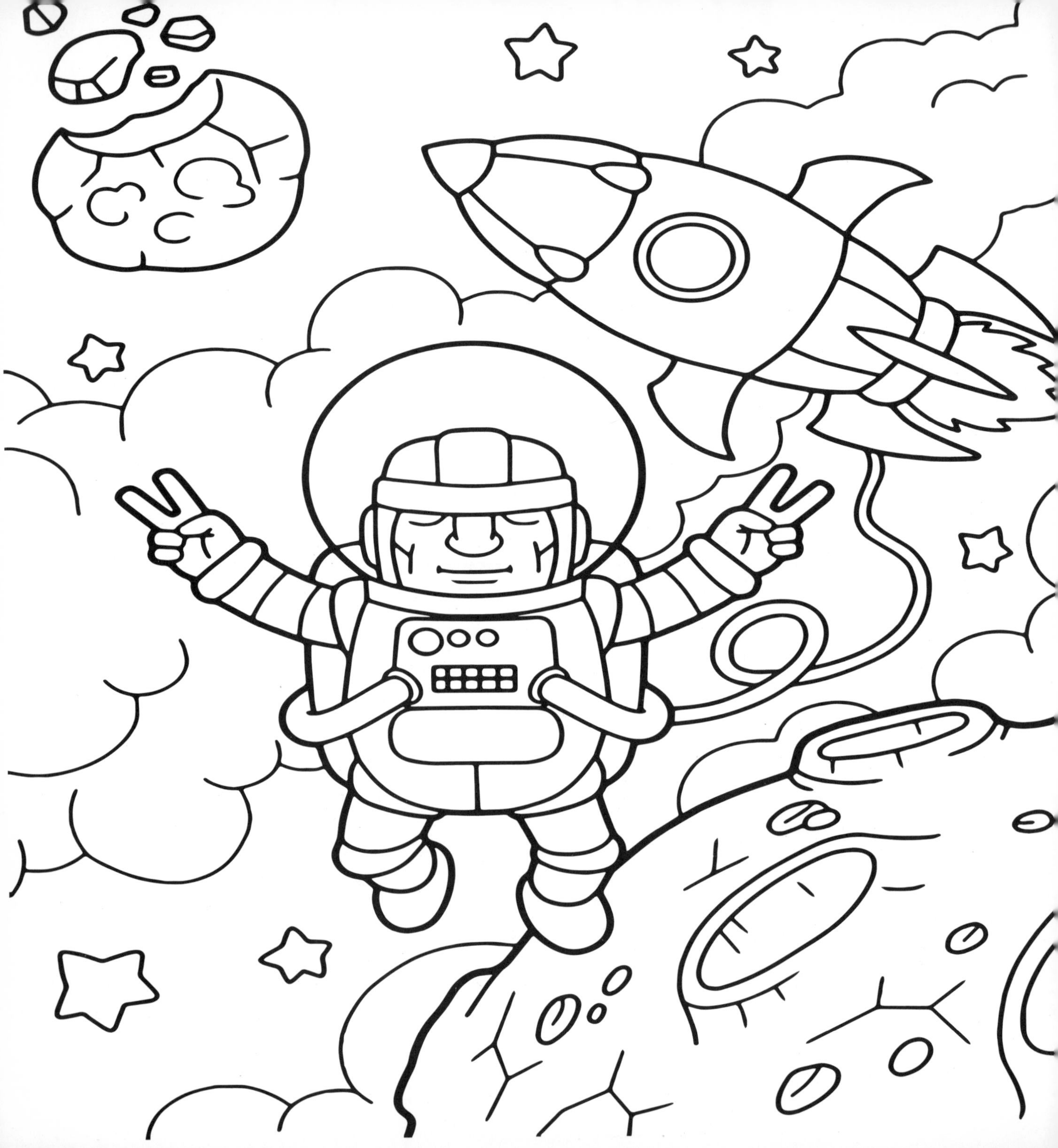

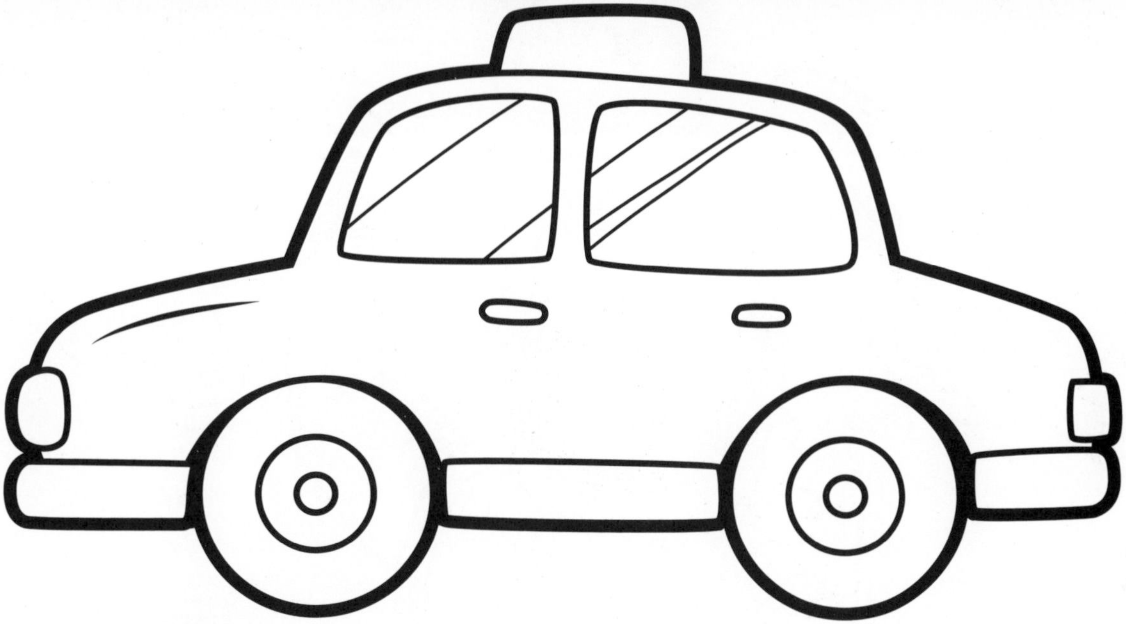

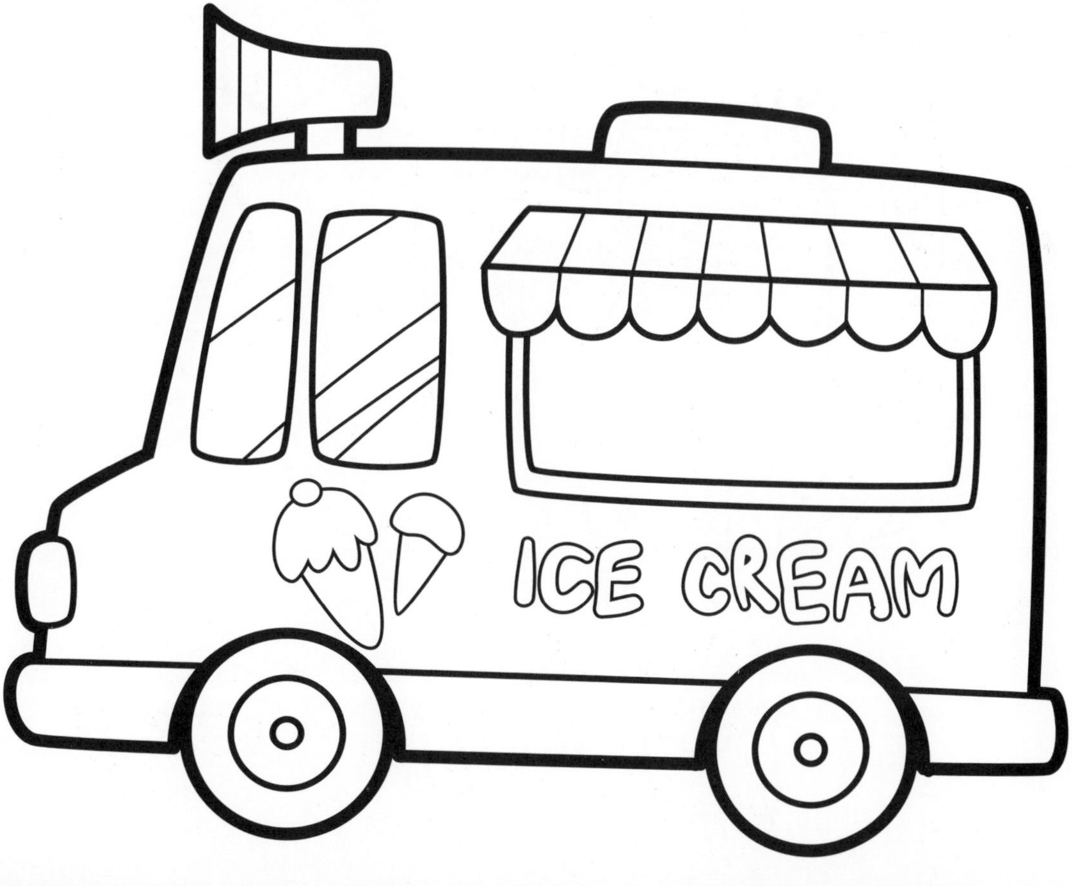
ICE CREAM

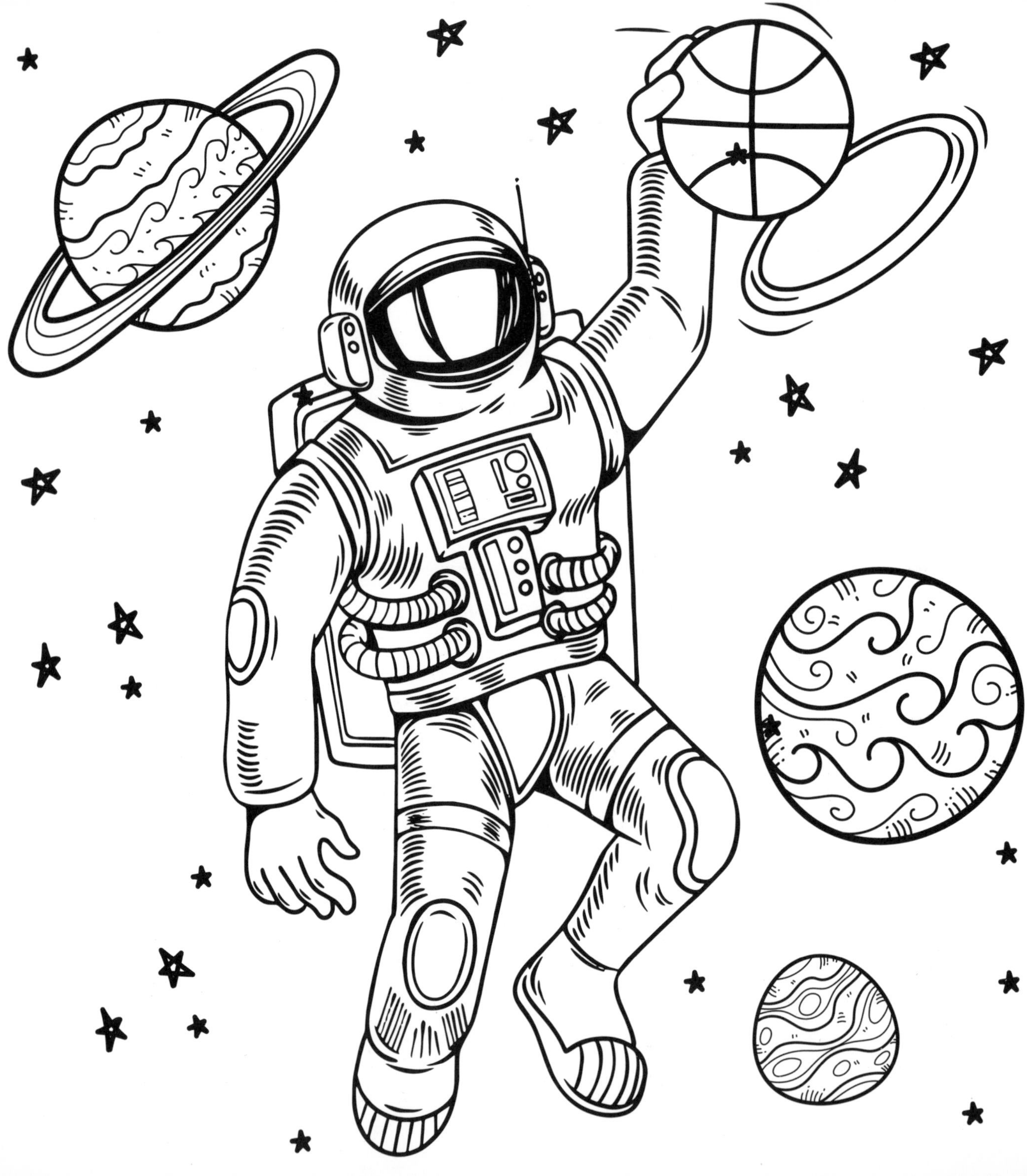

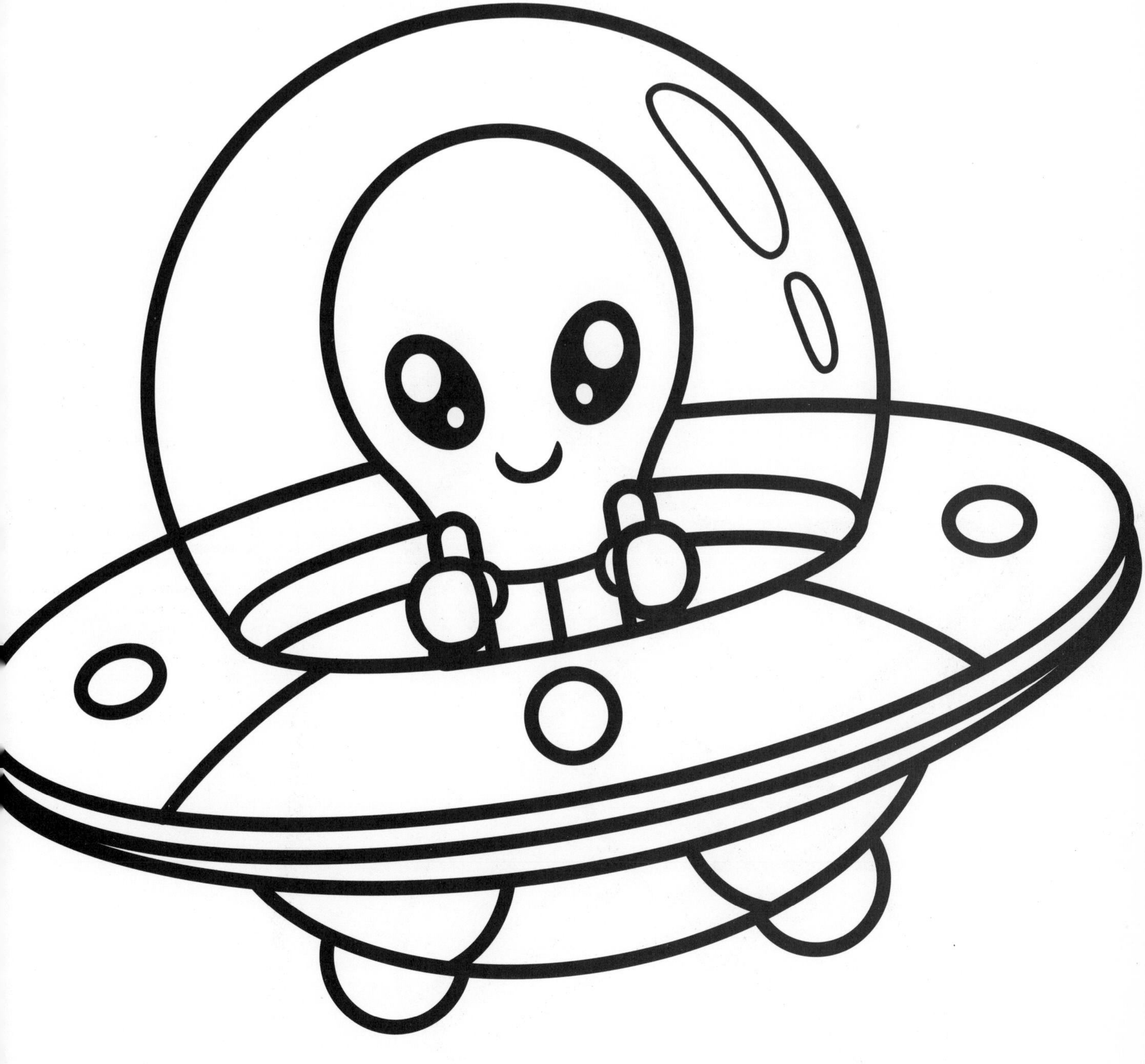

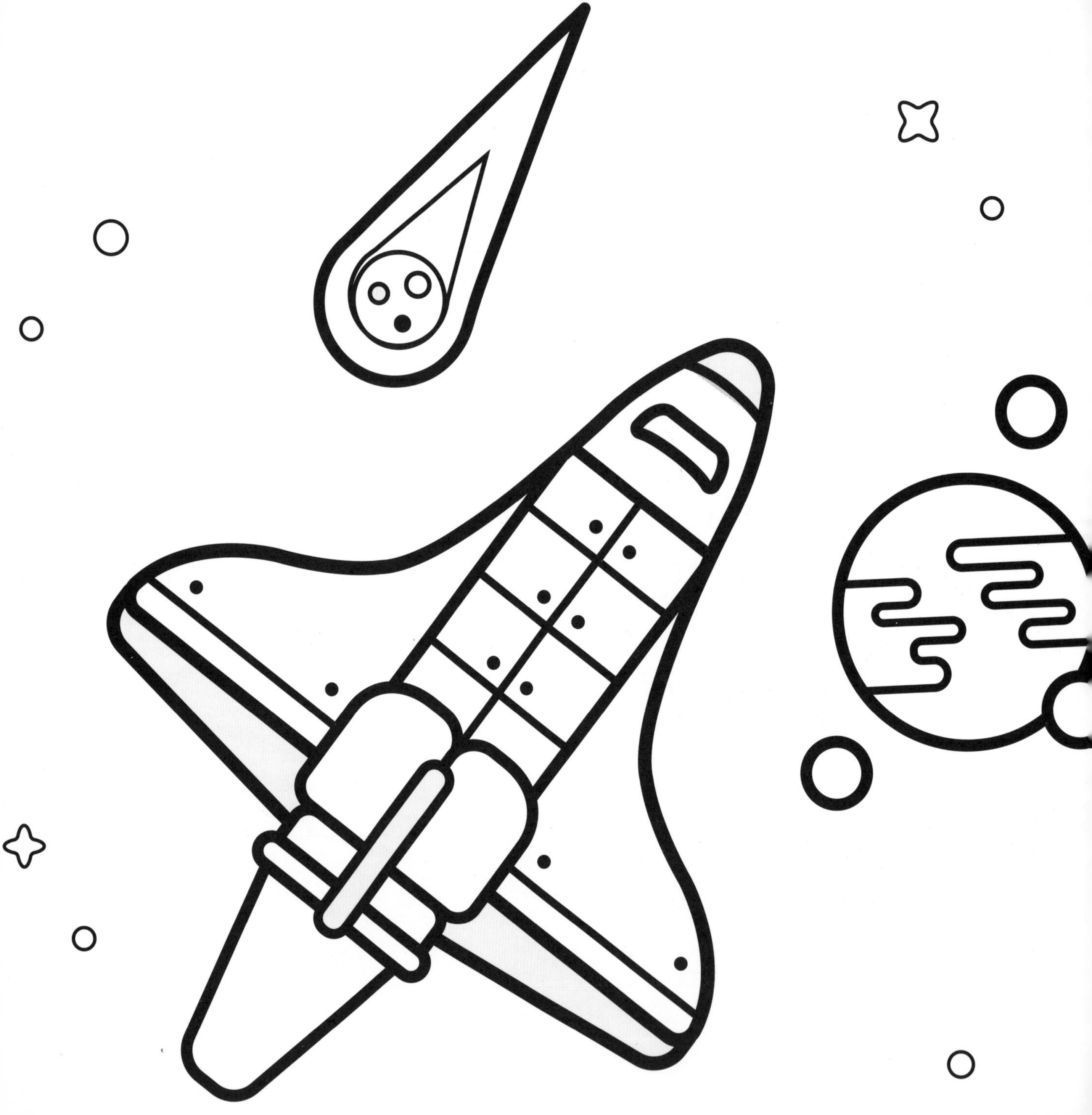

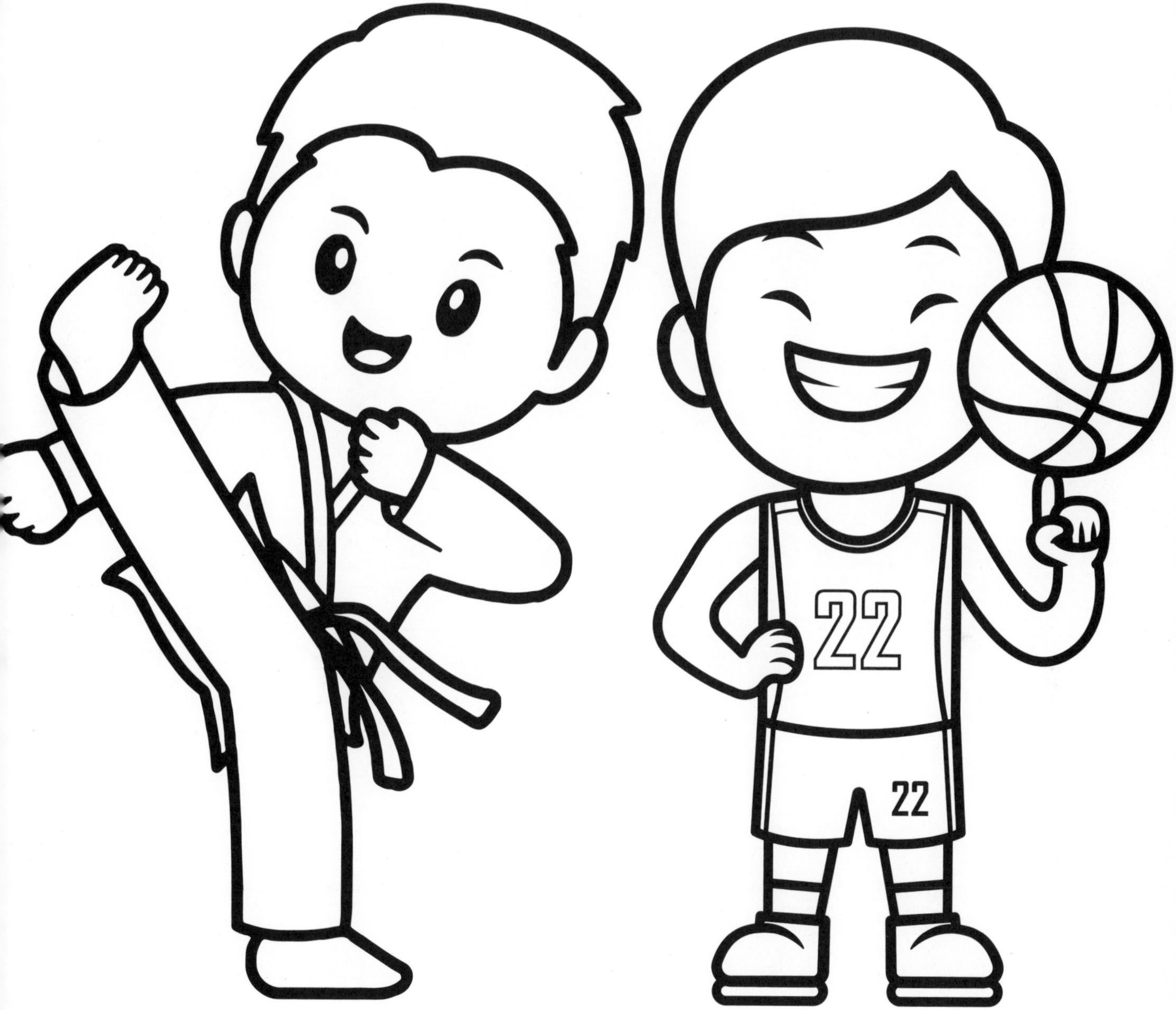
22
22

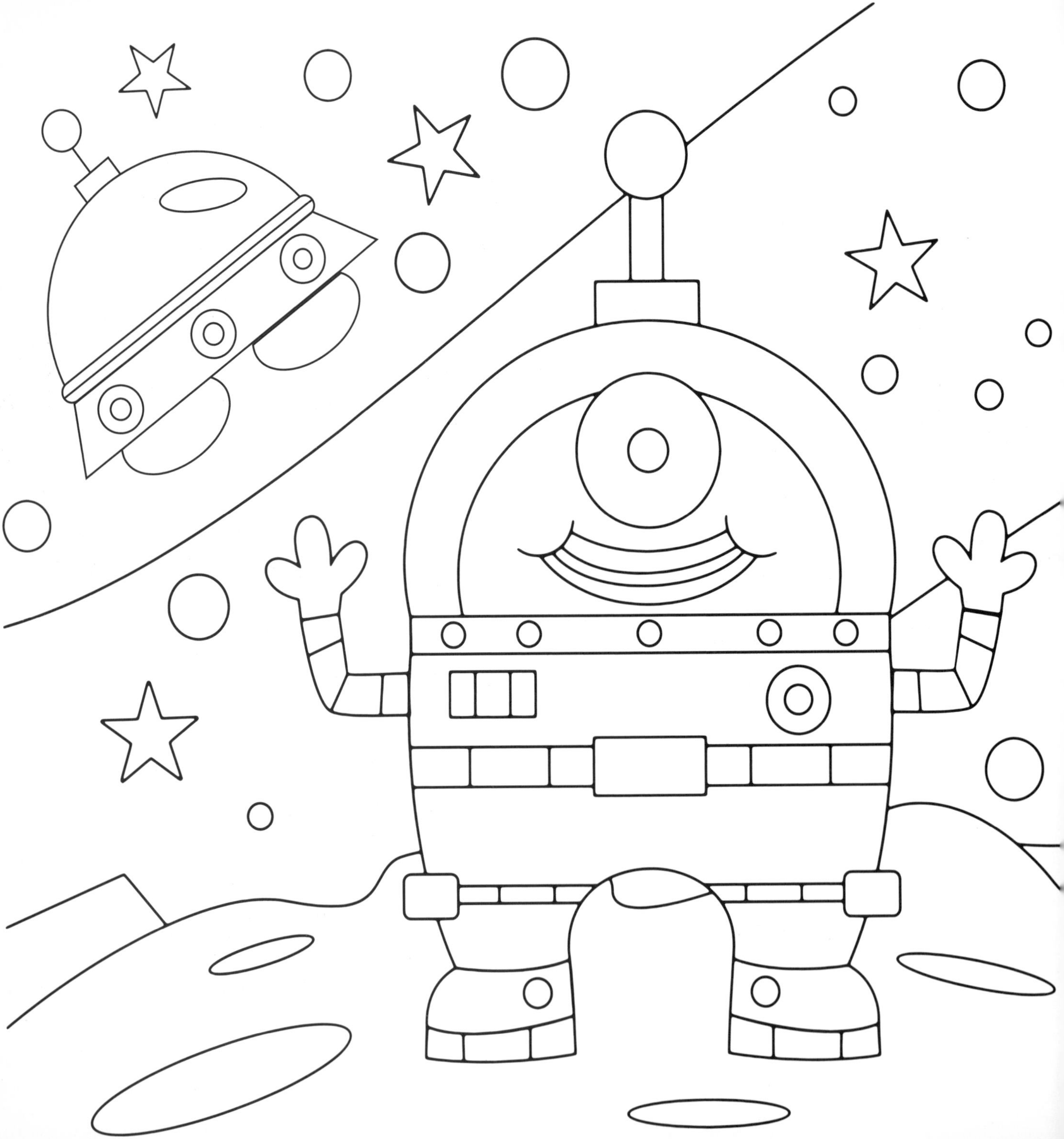

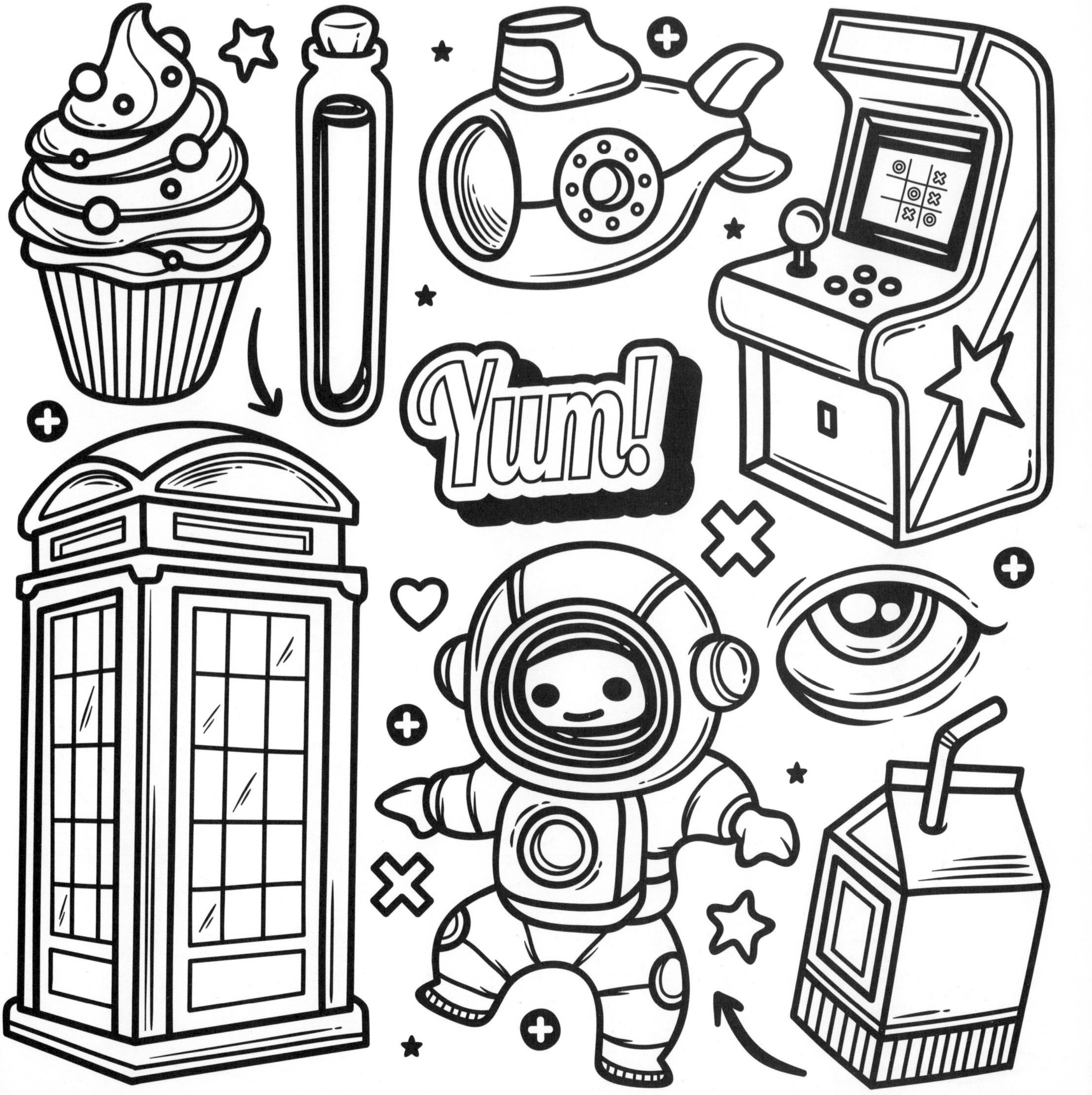
Yum!

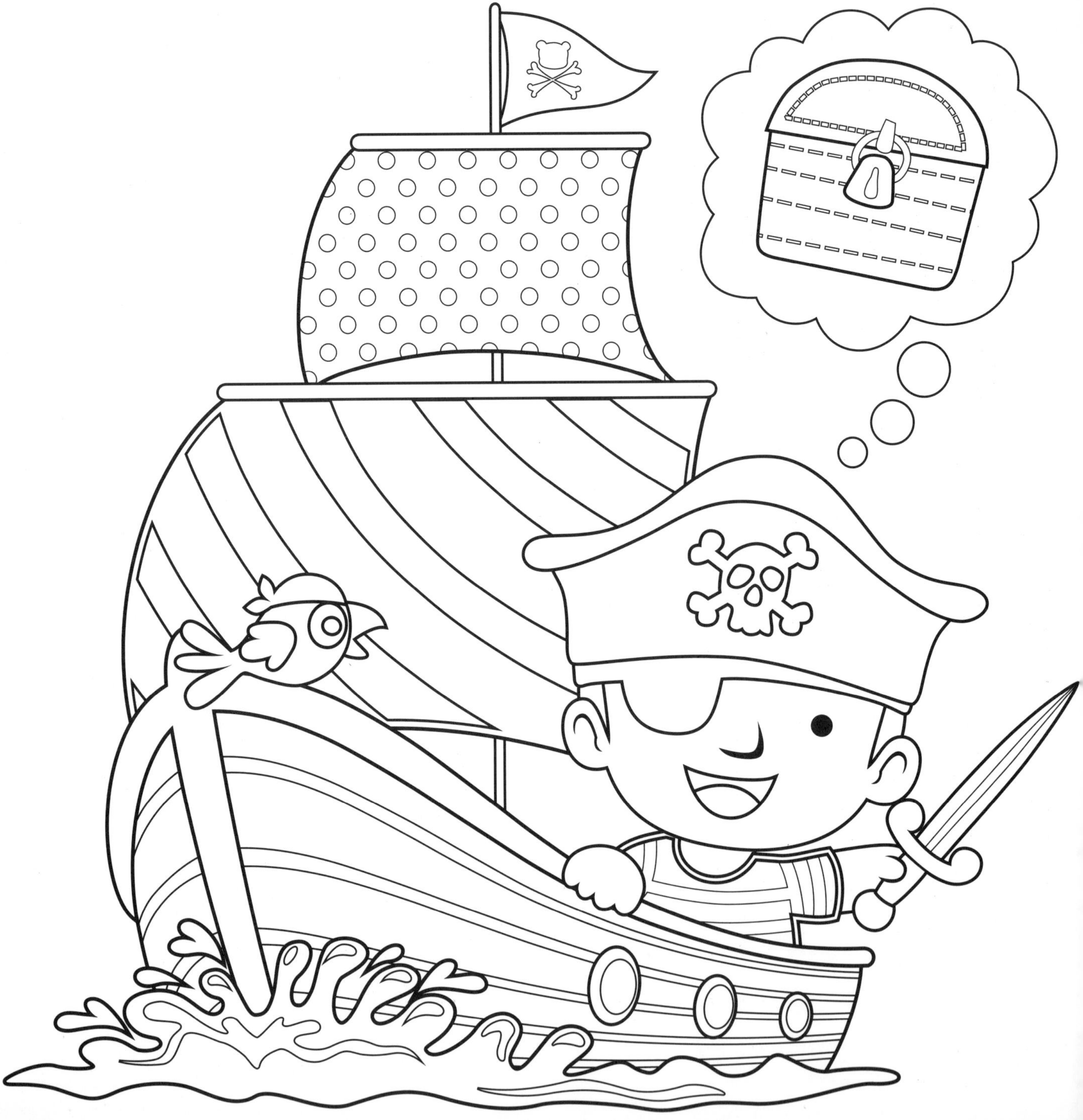

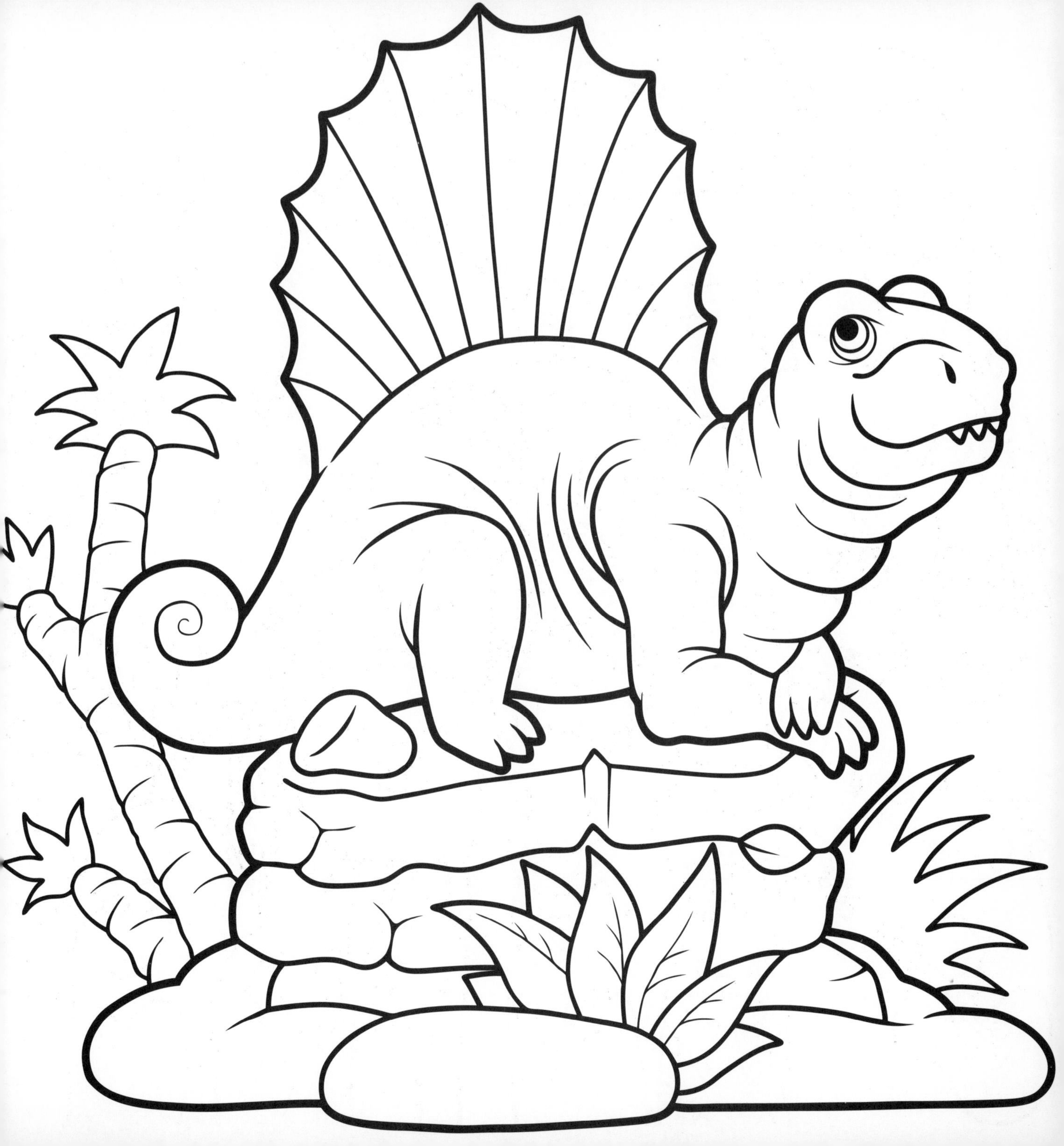

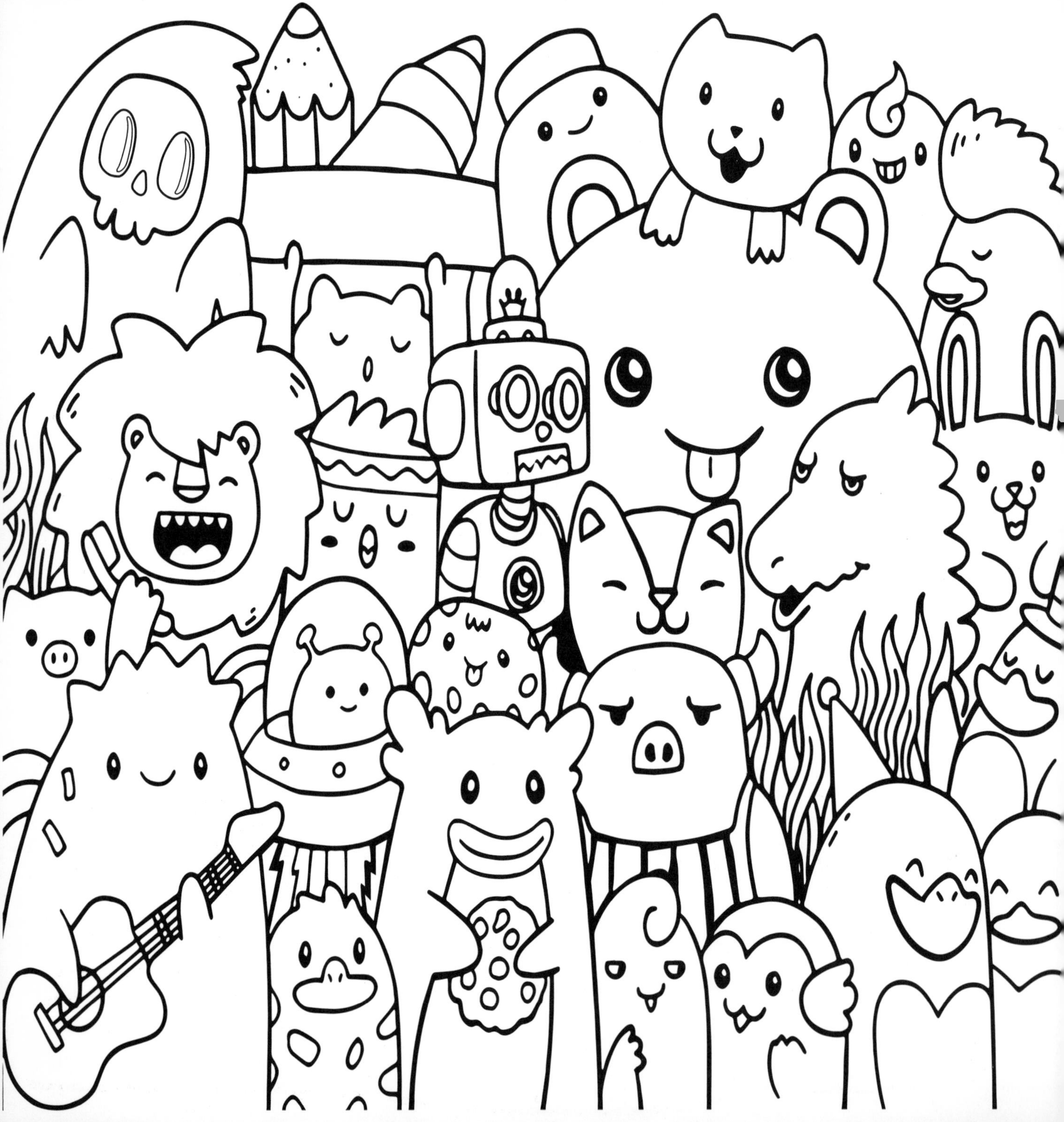

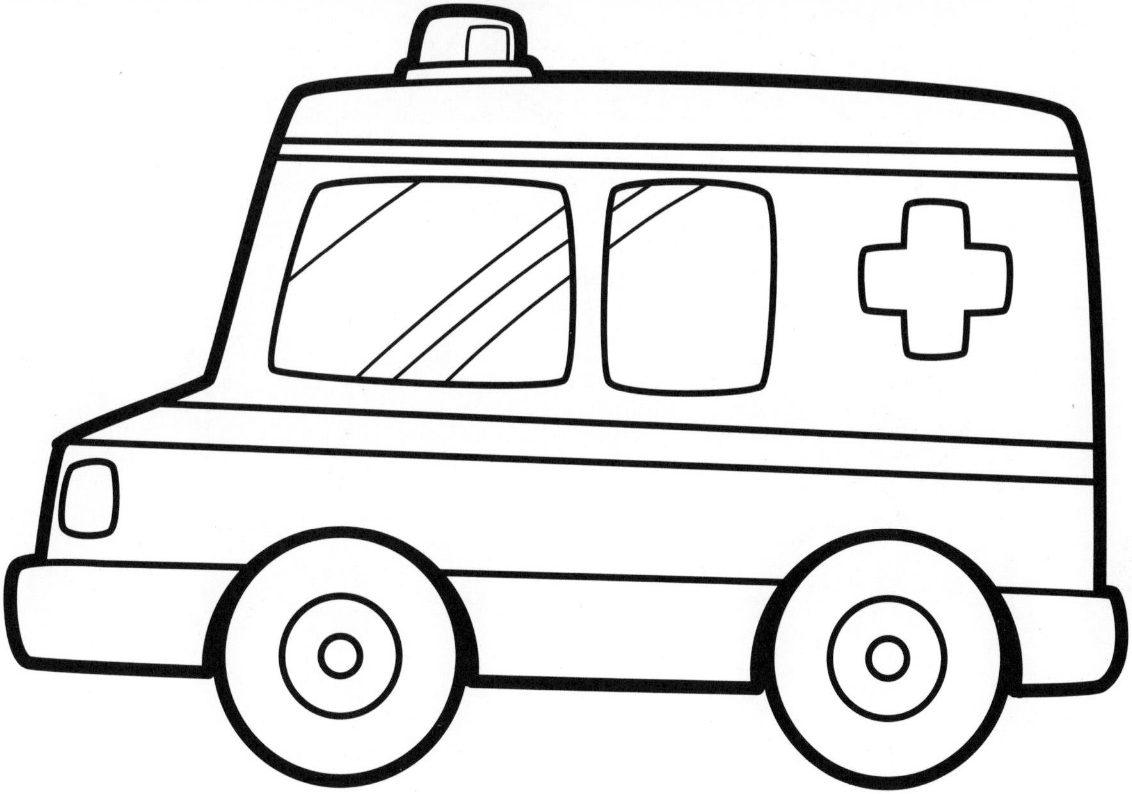

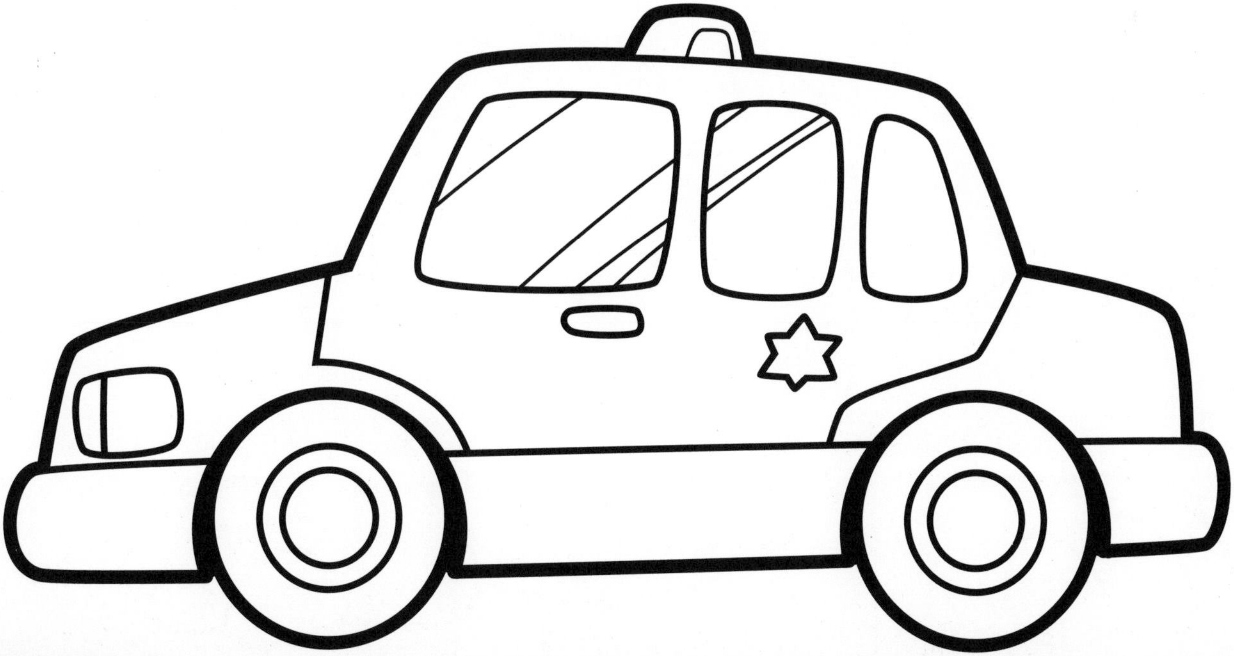

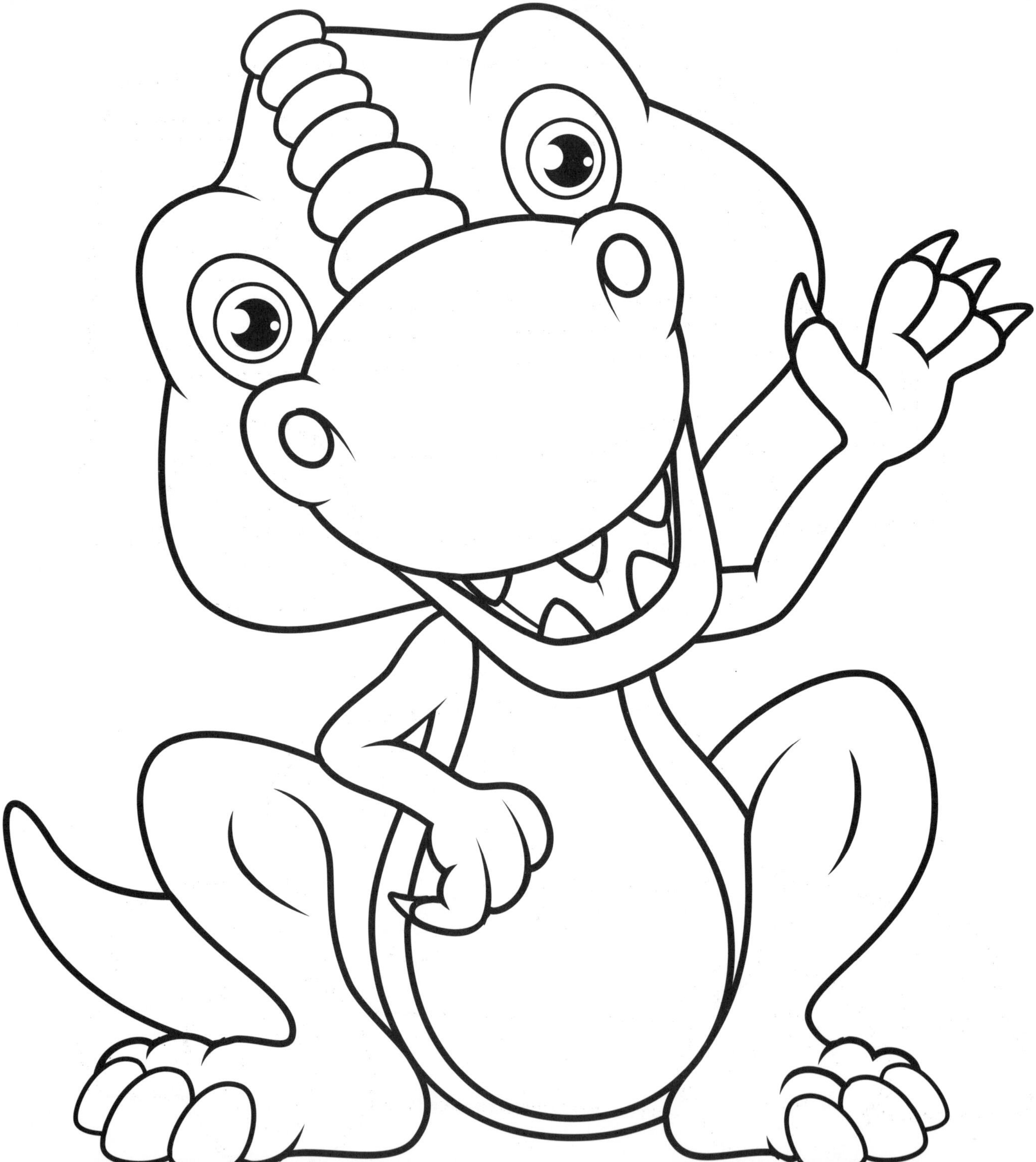

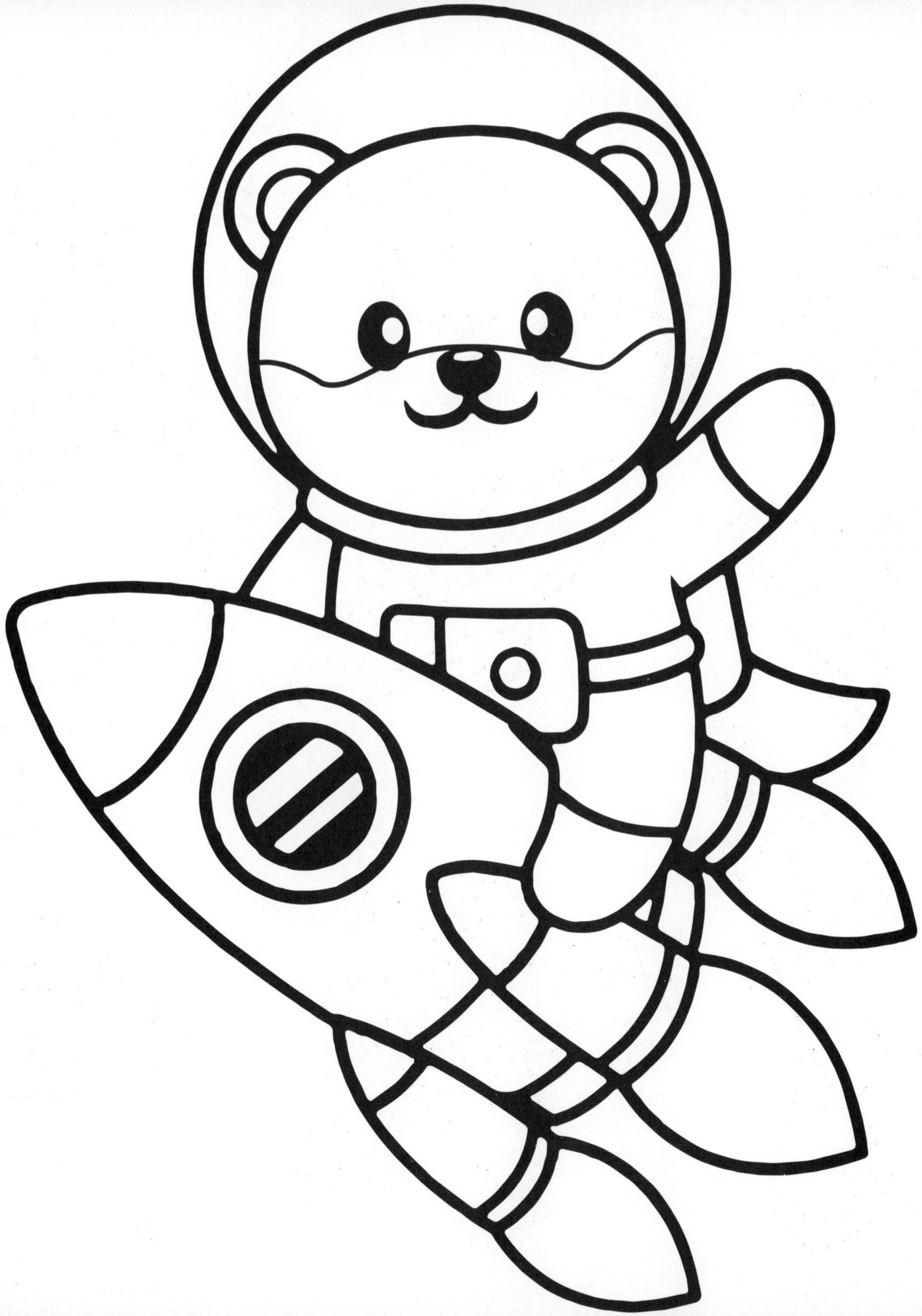

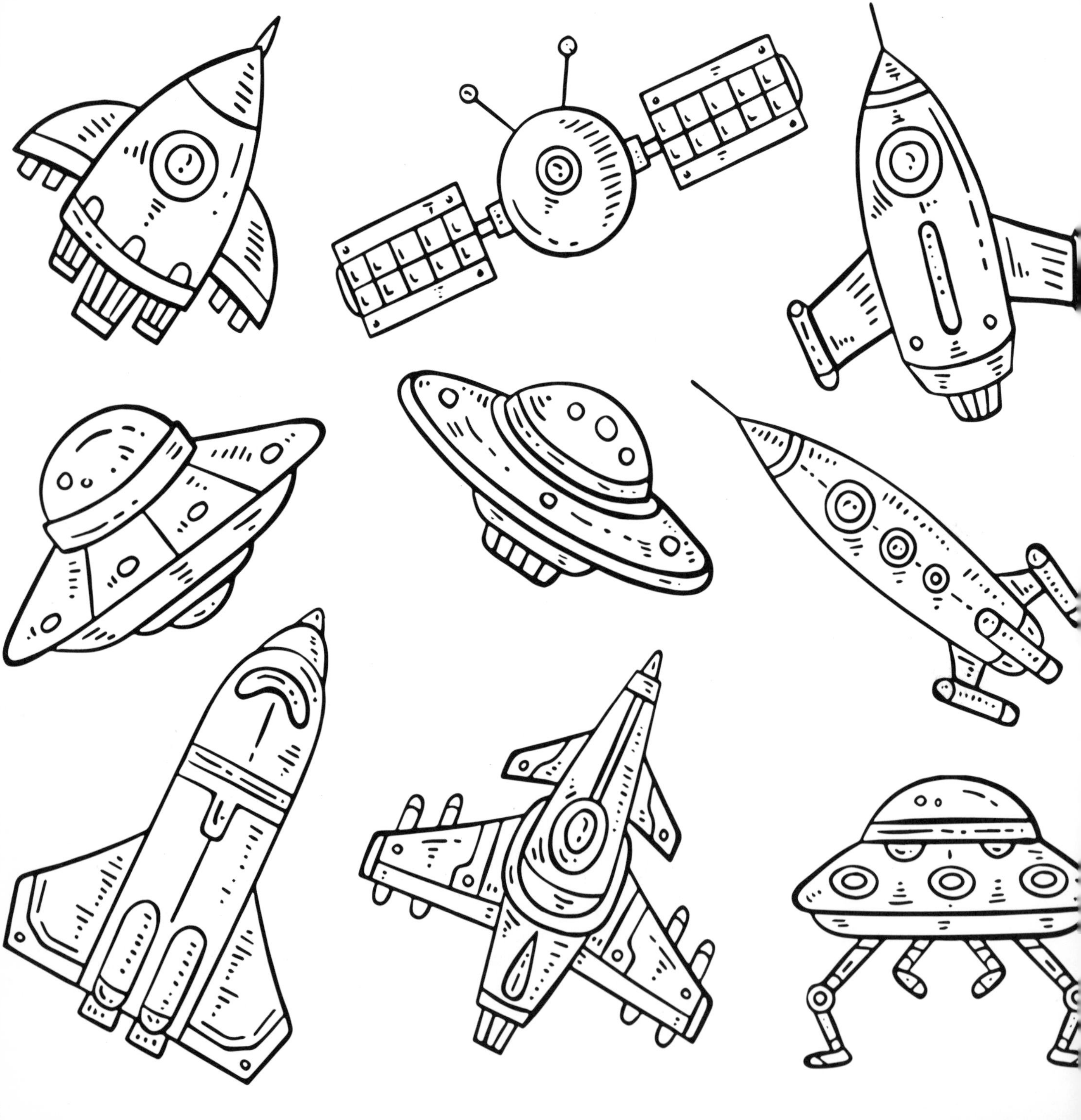

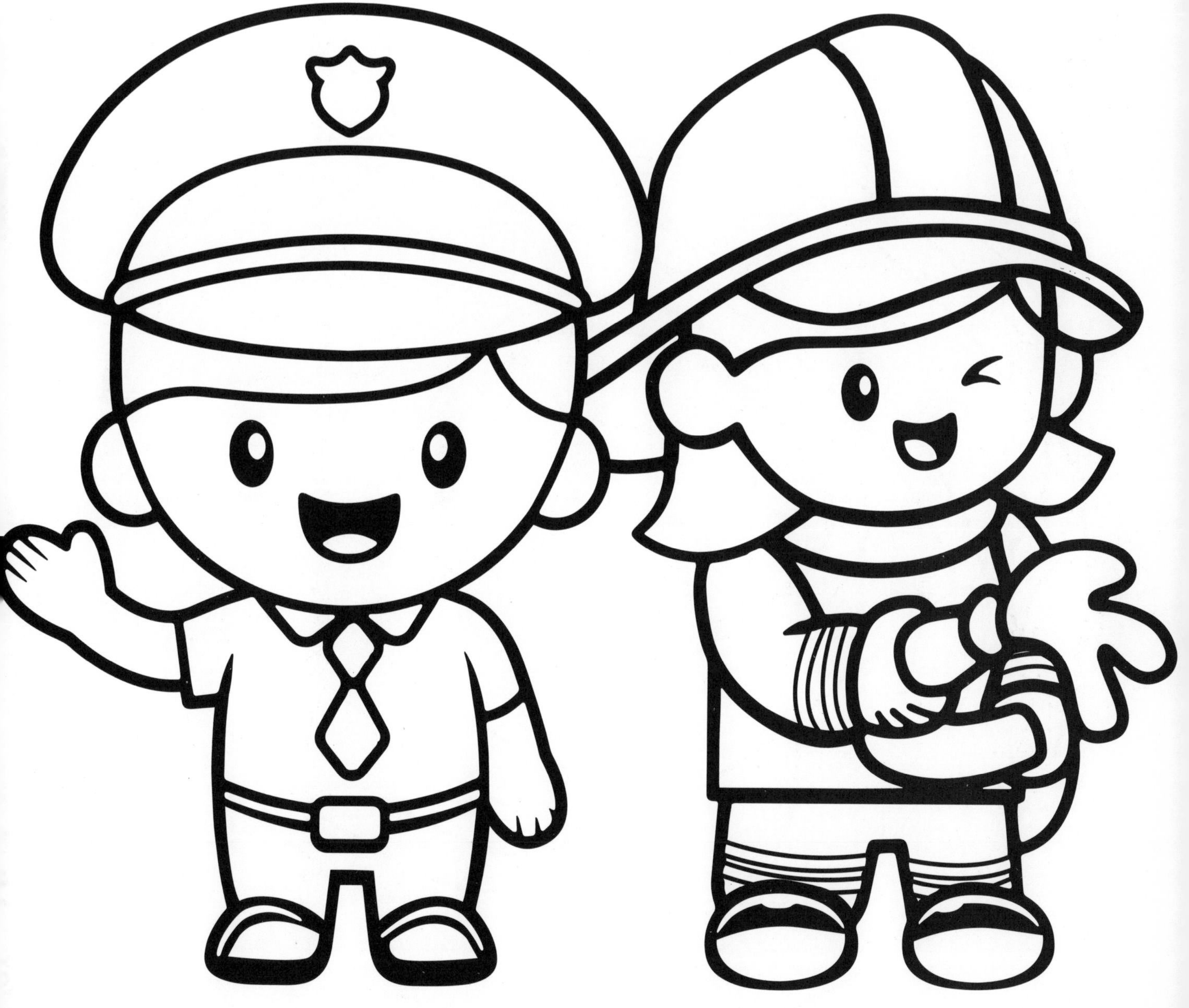

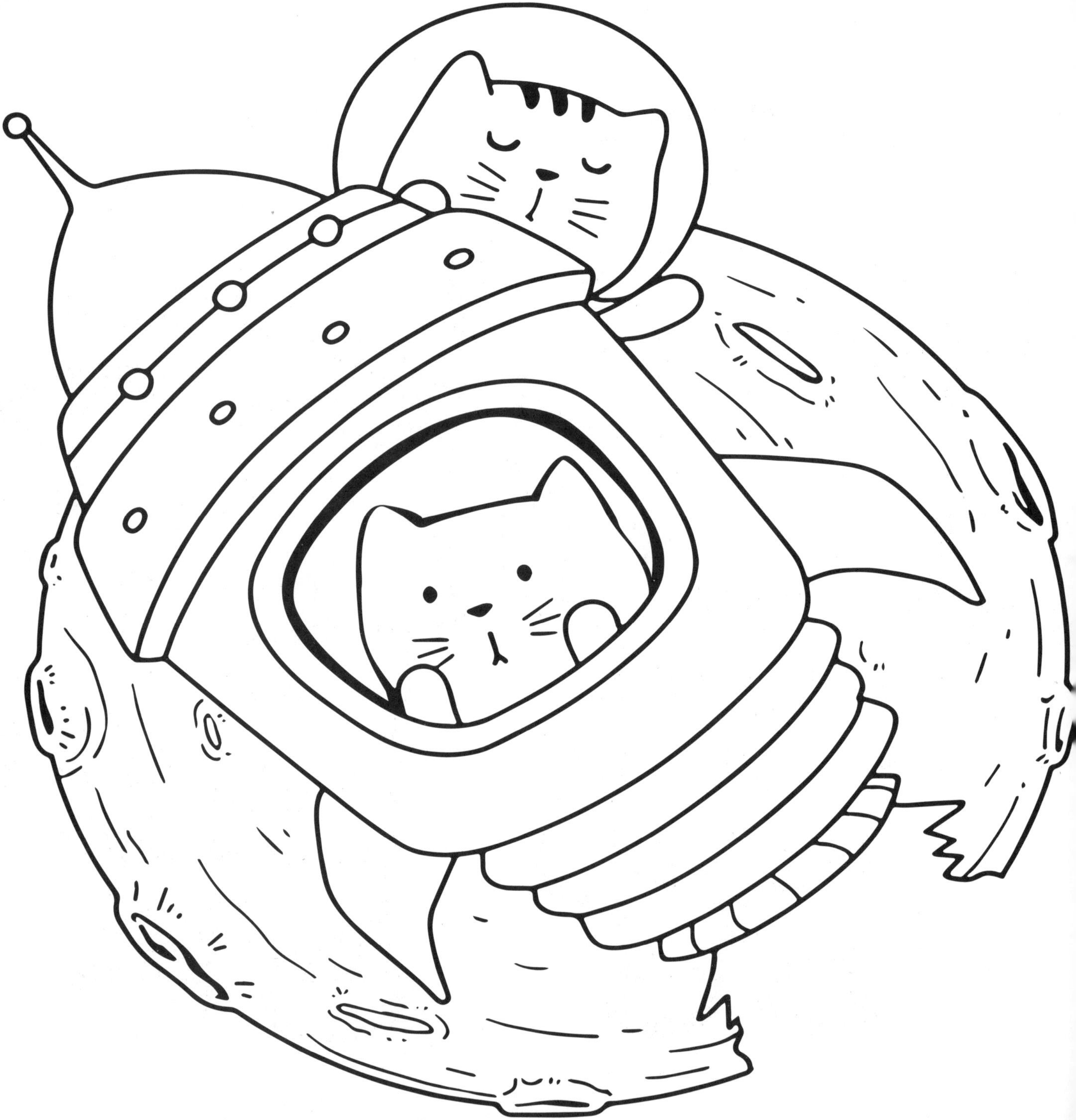

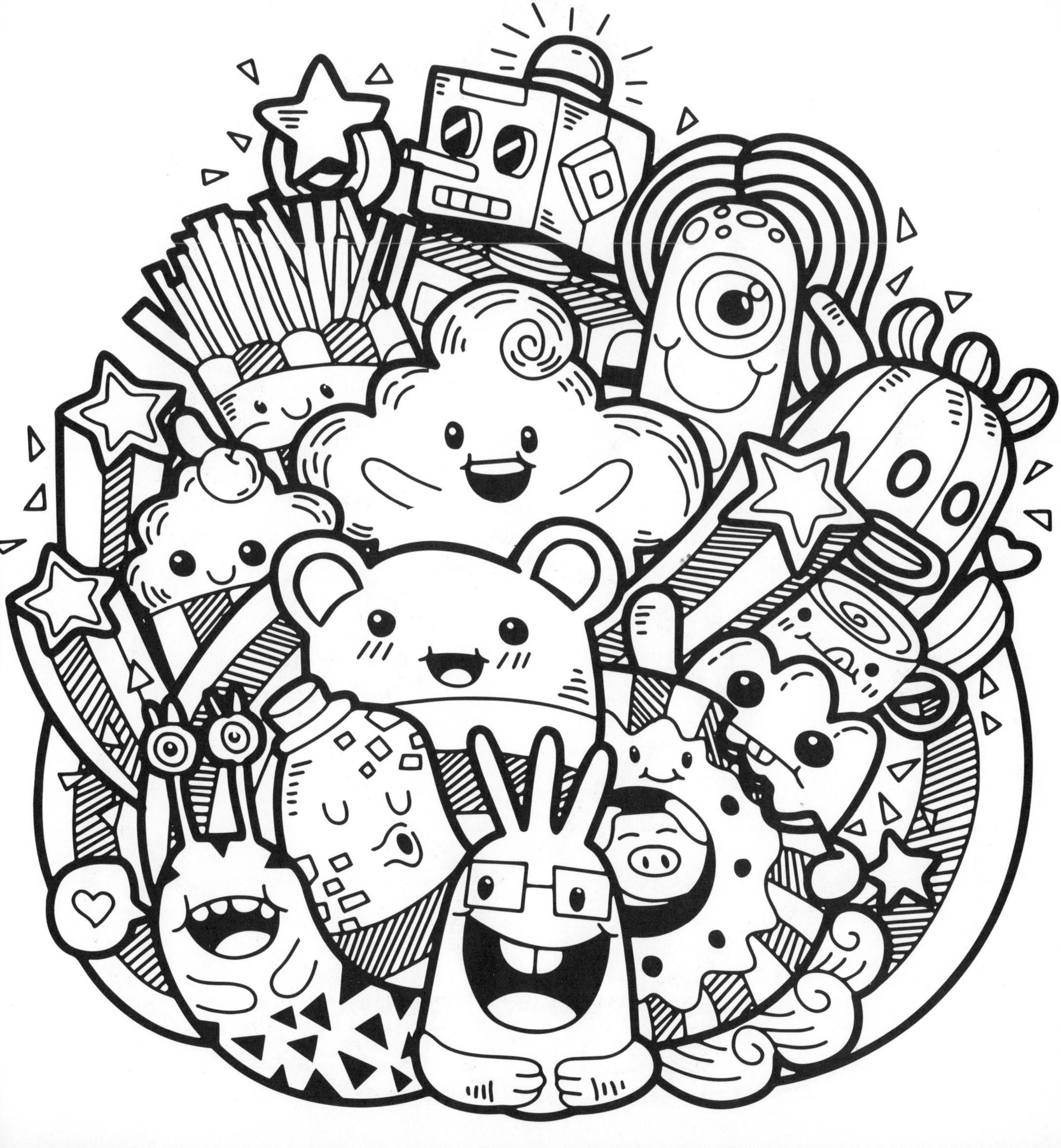

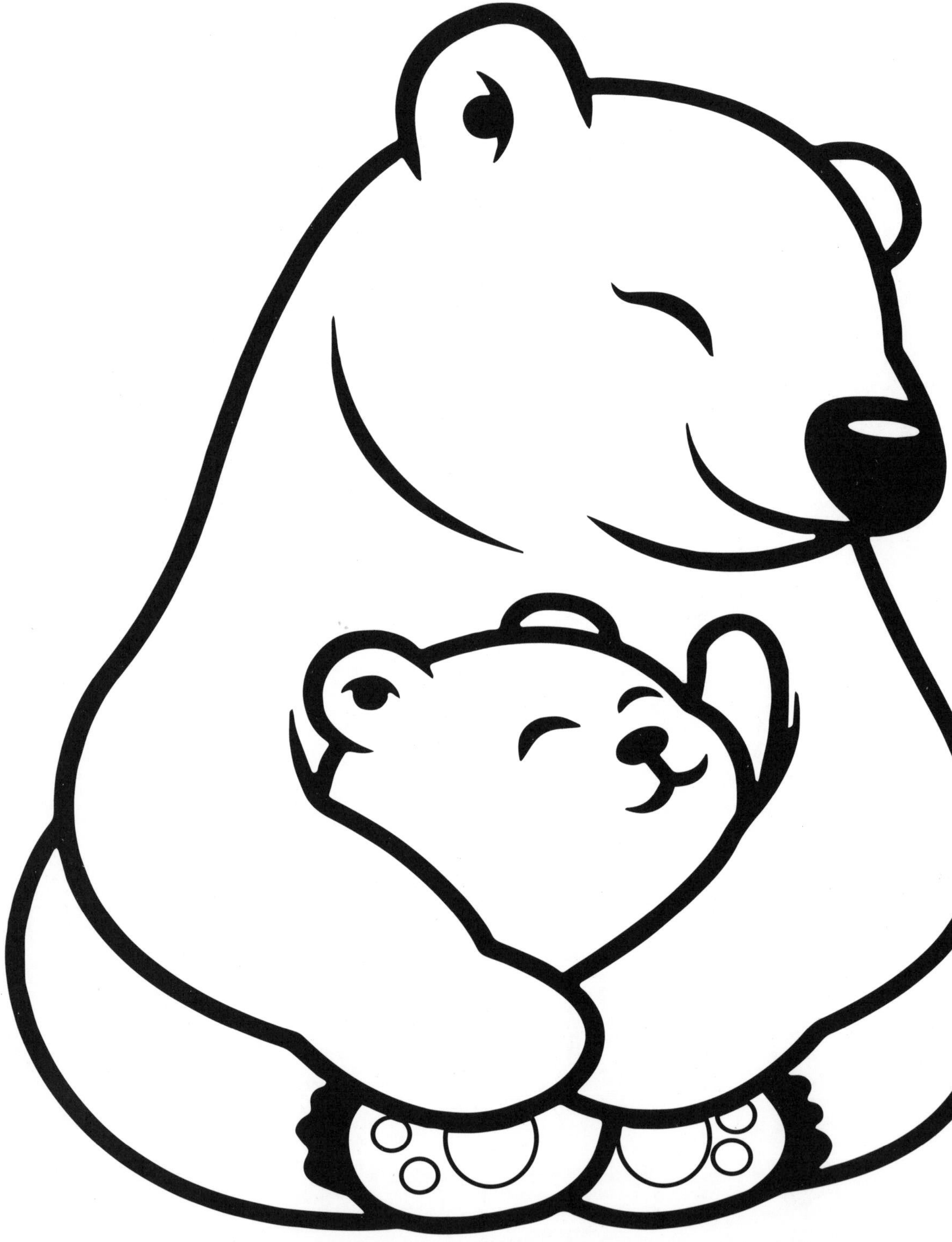

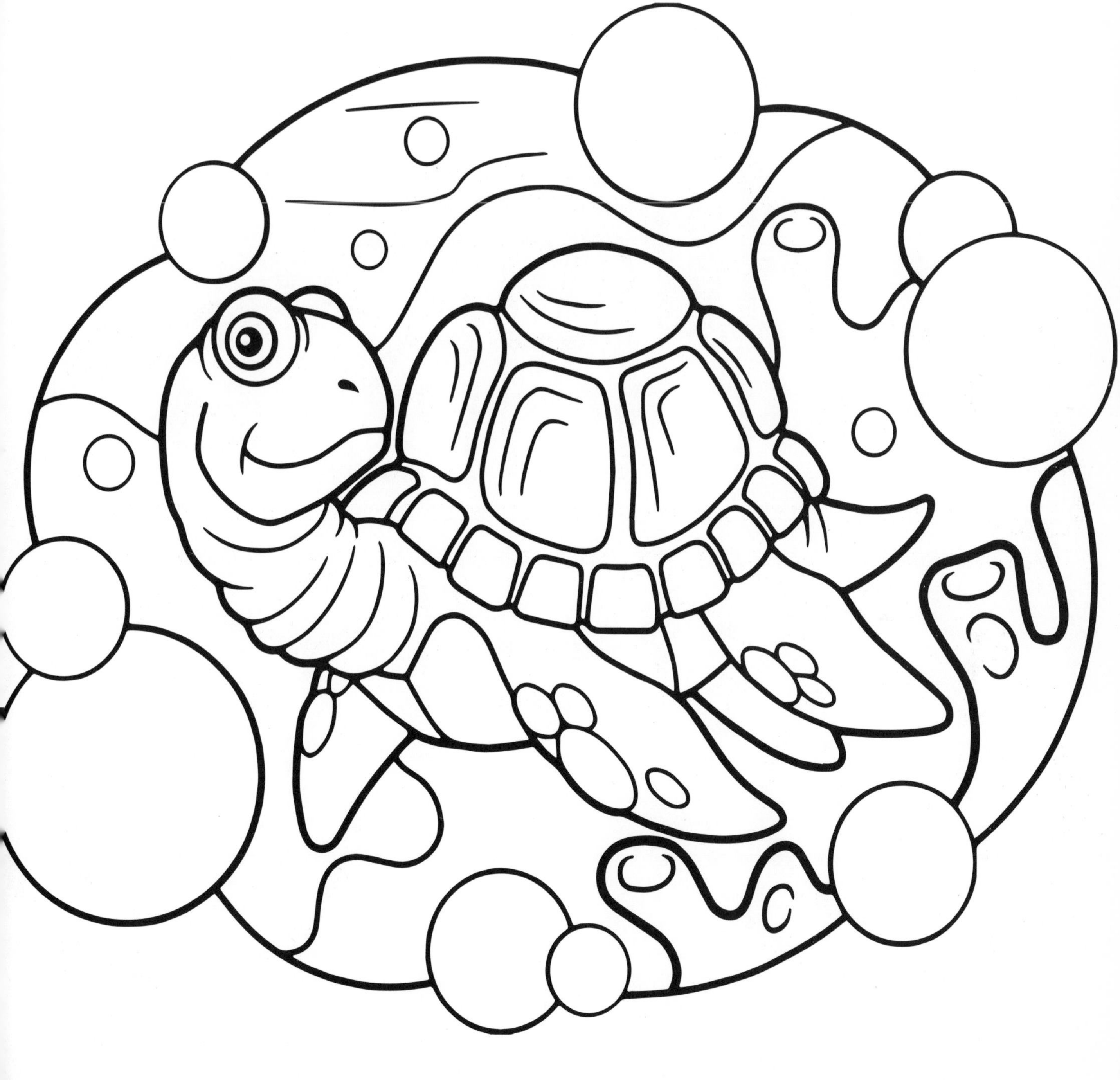

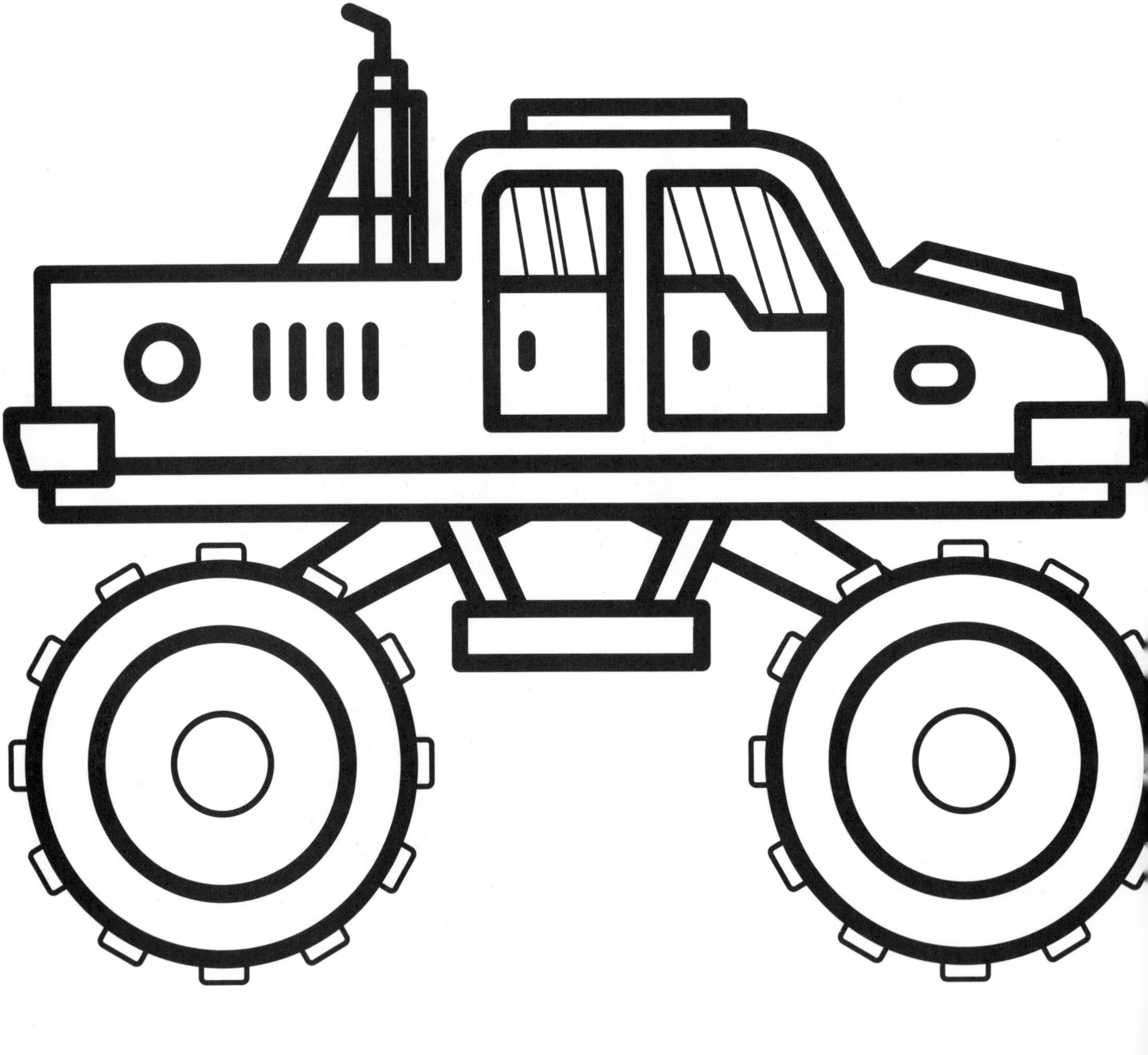

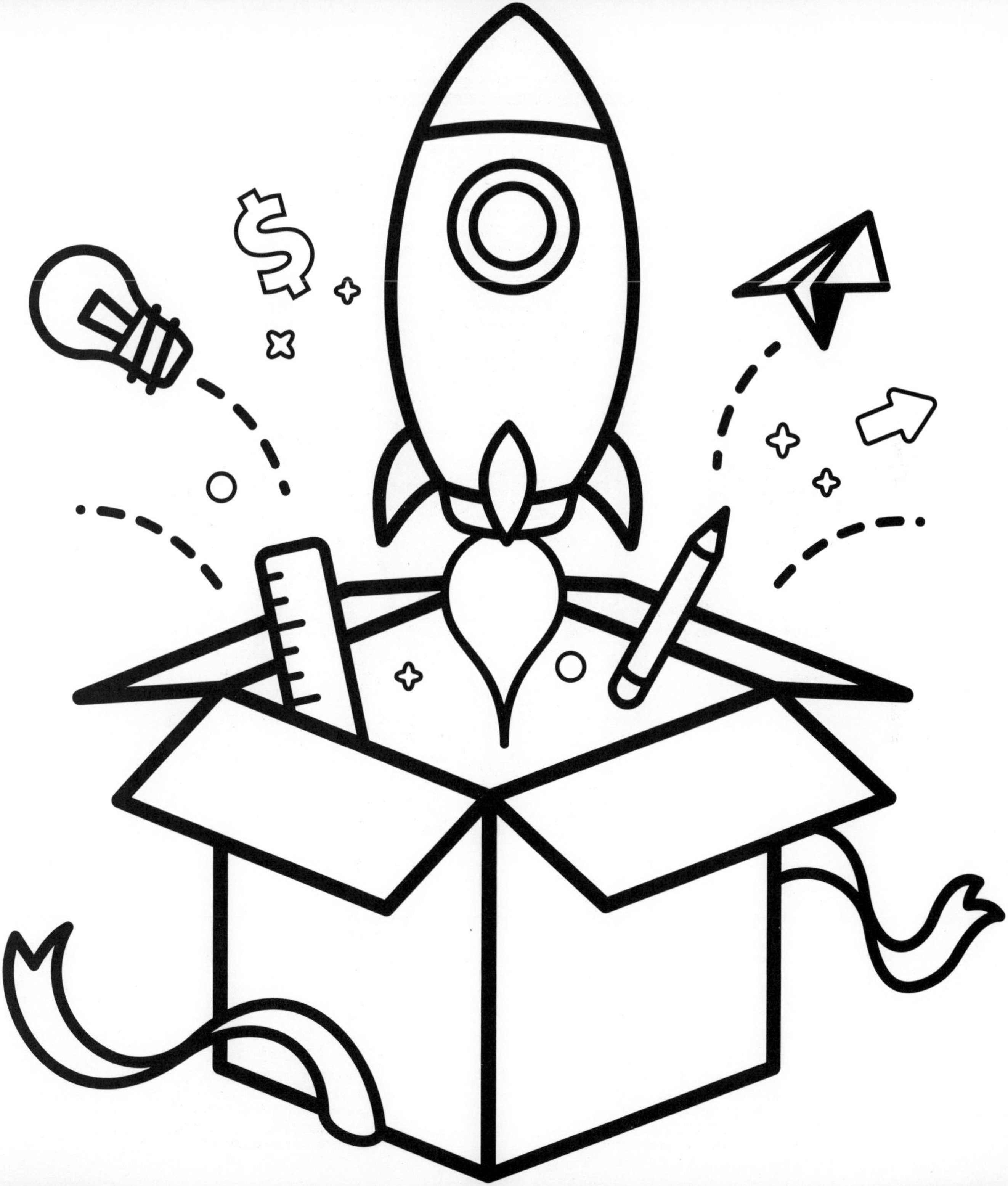

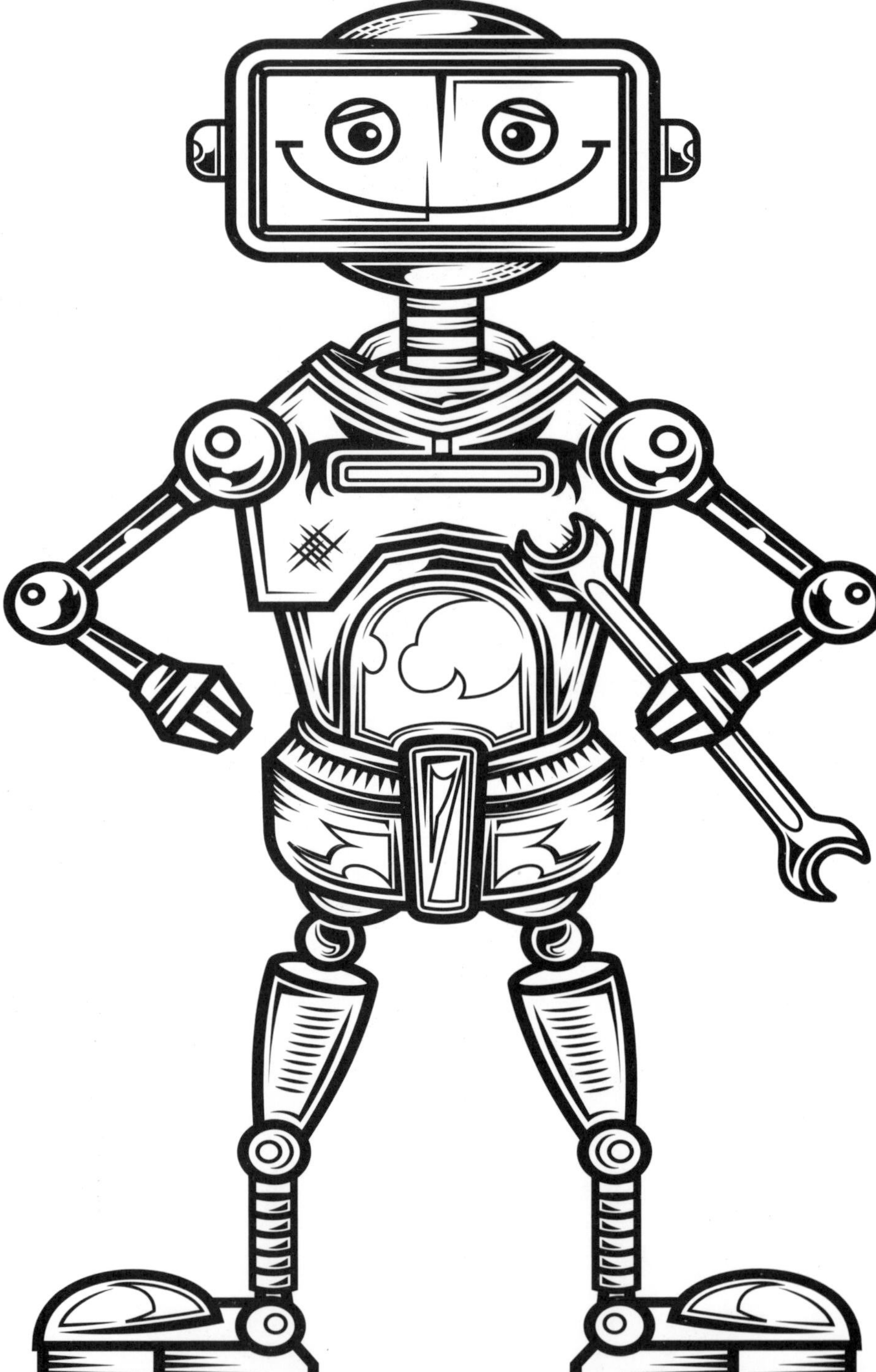

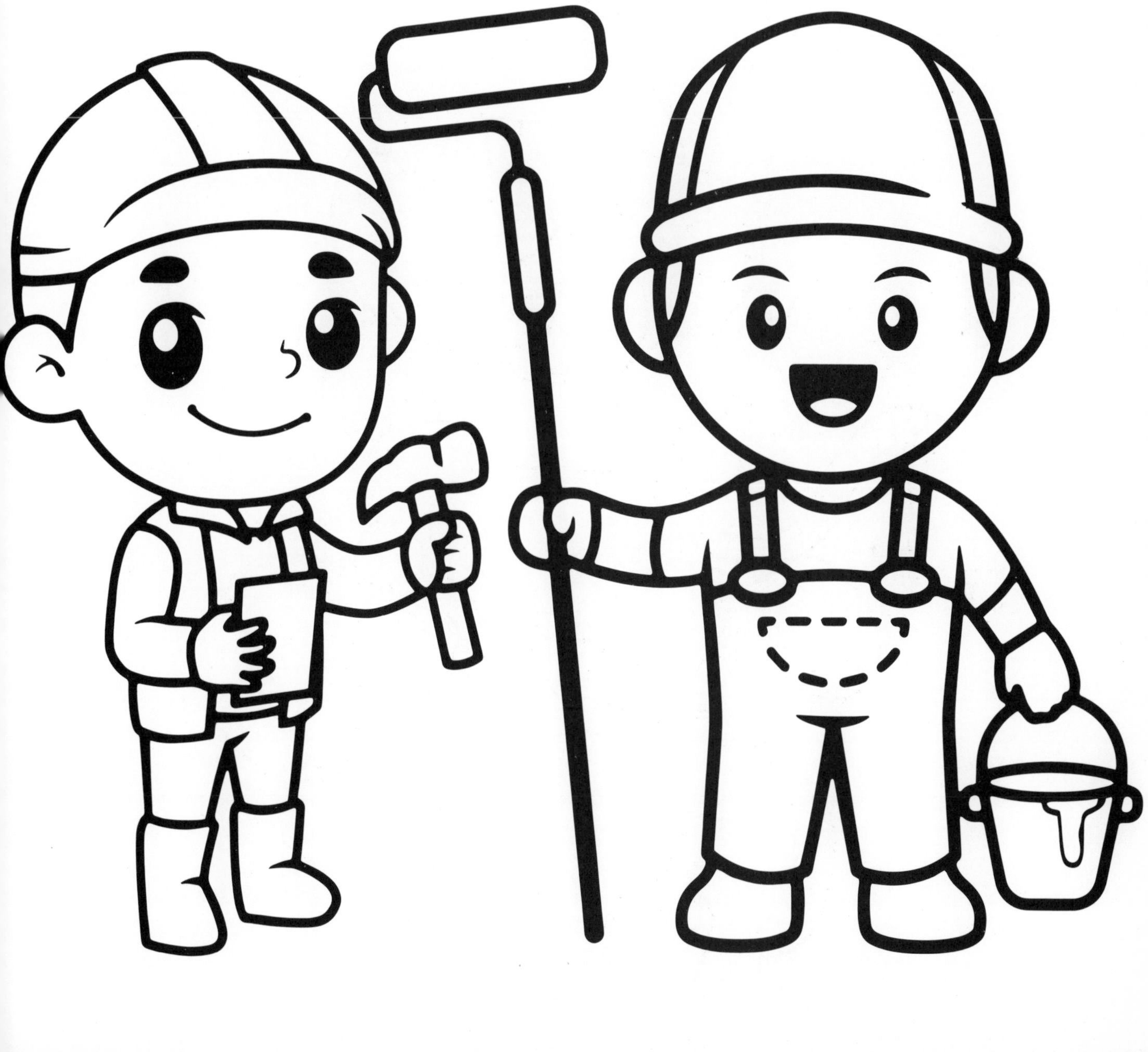

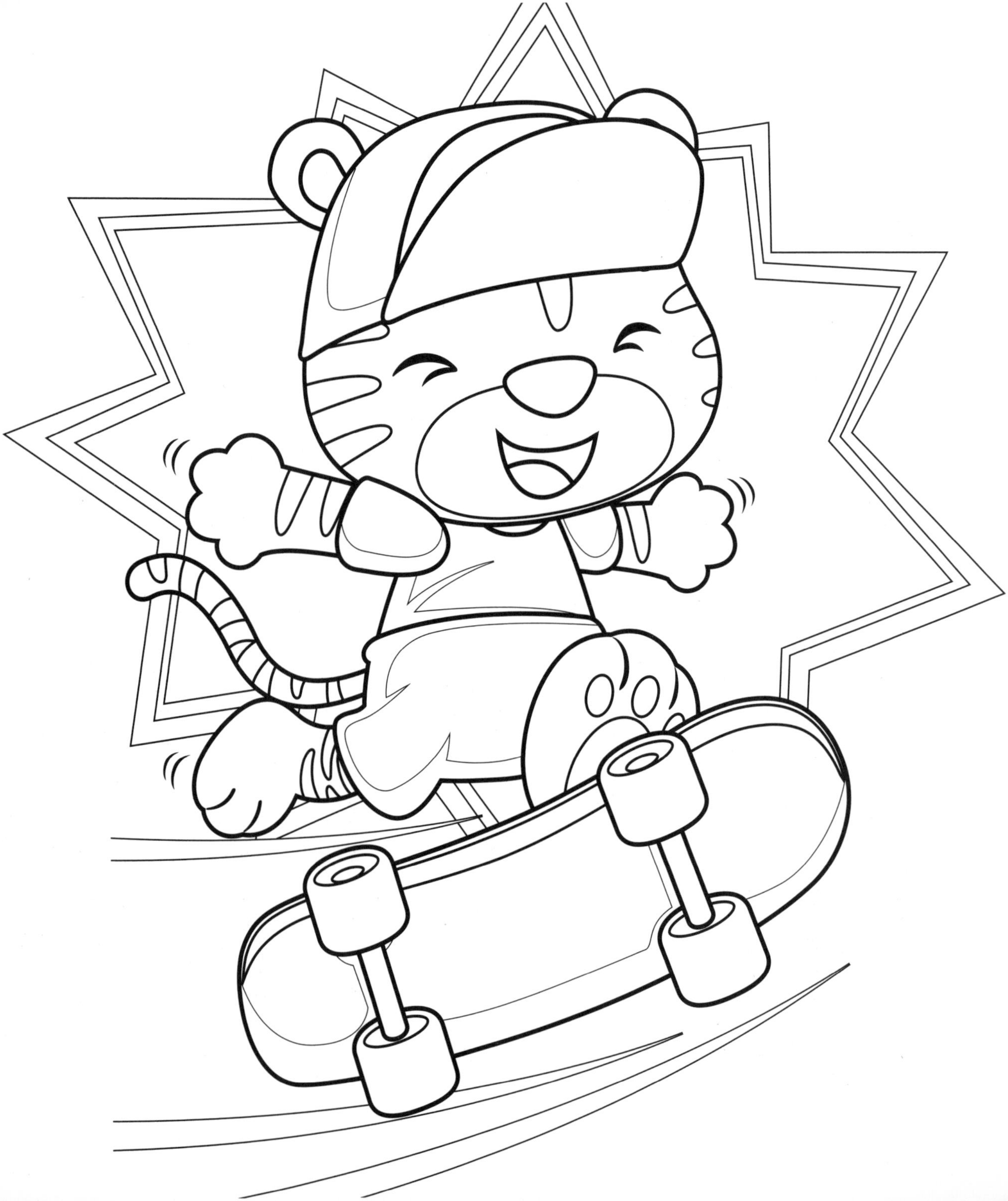

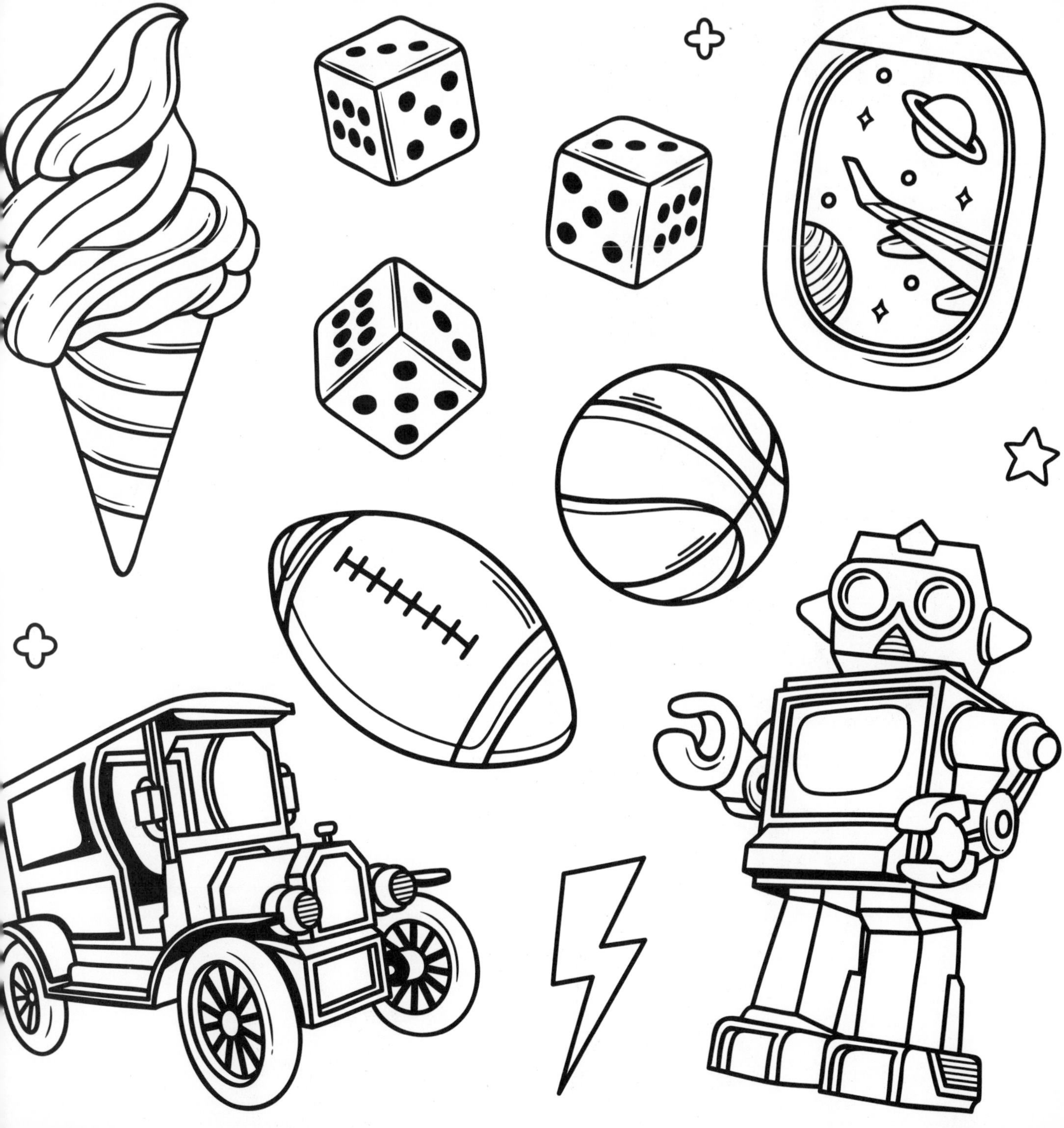

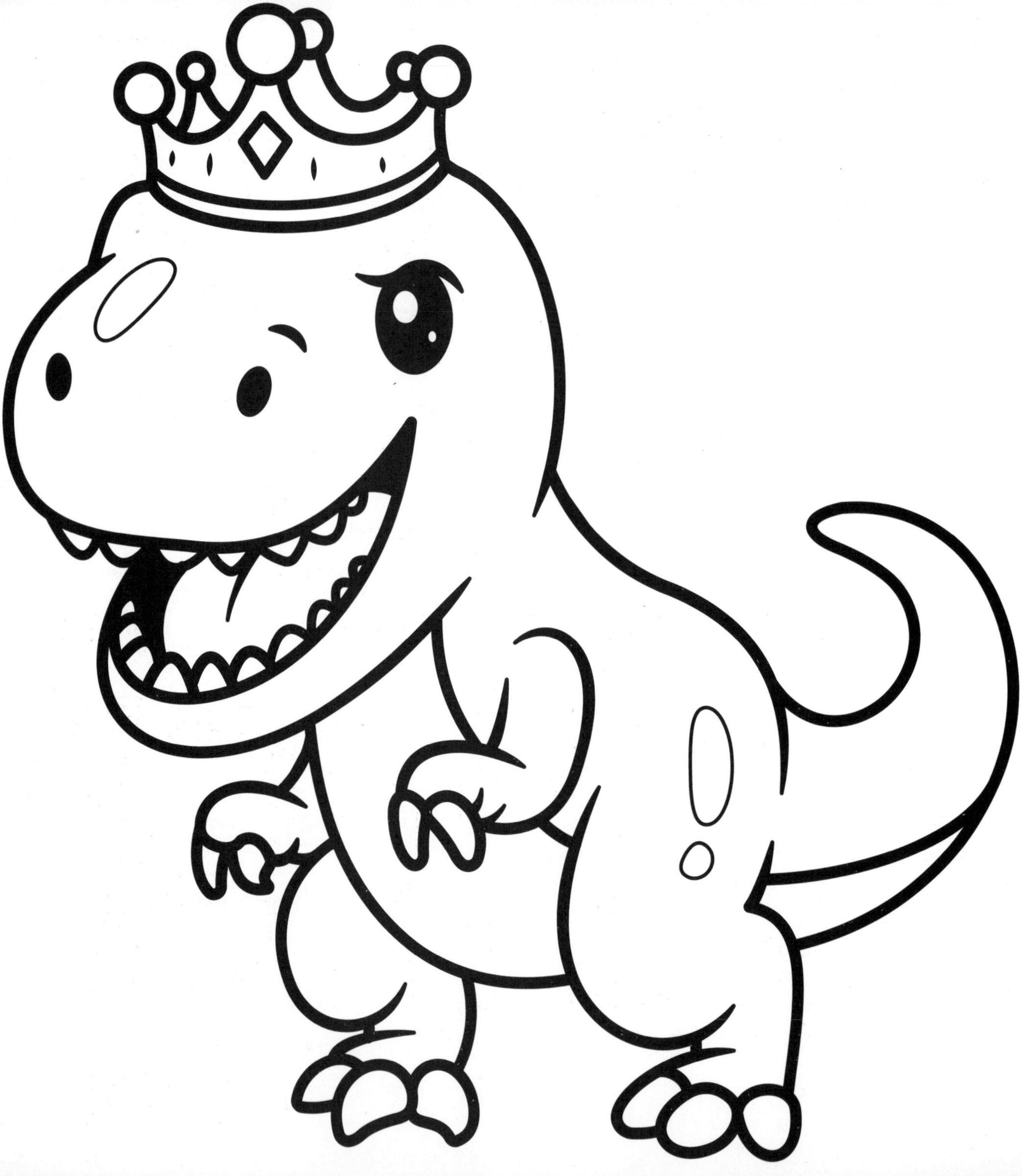